The NPO Dilemma

HR and Organizational Challenges in Non-Profit Organizations

Tim McConnell

The NPO Dilemma

HR and Organizational Challenges in Non-Profit Organizations

Tim McConnell

in cooperation with

DataMotion Publishing, LLC

New York

The NPO Dilemma: HR and Organizational
Challenges in Non-Profit Organizations

Library of Congress Control Number: 2012933202

ISBN: 978-1-937299-02-6

DataMotion Publishing, LLC
1019 Fort Salonga Road, Suite 10-333
Northport, NY 11768-2209
www.datamotionpublishing.com

Some men see things as they are and say *why*?

I dream things that never were and say *why not*?

Robert F. Kennedy

I love it when a plan comes together!

Hannibal, the A Team

Table of Contents

Forward 3

About the Author 7

Warning–Disclaimer 11

~~~~~~~~~~

Chapter 1: Introduction 13

Chapter 2: HR Strategy 27

What is it, and Why do You Need One?

Chapter 3: Organization Design 45

Is Your Organization Aligned to Support its Vision and Mission?

Chapter 4: Staffing 73

Who's on First?

Chapter 5: Compensation 97

Show Me the Money

Chapter 6: Employee Retention 125

Will the People You Hire Stay?

Chapter 7: Succession Planning......................137

Who's Next?

Chapter 8: Human Resources Outsourcing.....147

Buy or Rent?

Appendix I: How to Speak HR..........................153

An NPO Reader's Guide to the Mystical World
of HR Speak

**Appendix II: The Top Ten Mistakes in HR
Management**..157

Tales from the Front Lines of HR Consulting

About DataMotion Publishing 167

Forward

Finally – a book that is specific to human resources and organizational management in the non-profit sector. There are hundreds, if not thousands, of books that have been written about managing human resources in the private sector and there are some books that address HR management in both the public and the non-profit sectors, but we are indeed "different."

The content of this book is great; highly readable. I seriously wish I had a reference like this twenty years ago.

This book acknowledges many of the realities and circumstances of the non-profit sector: that there are many small organizations with limited budgets (although there are some very large nonprofits with much greater capacity), that becoming an effective manager of people is often learned on the job, and that our bottom line is not measured in dollars and cents but in making a real difference in people's lives and in our communities.

This book is a true reflection of the author and how his firm works with nonprofits. They are experienced HR professionals who understand the context in which we work because so much of their business has focused on nonprofits over the last ten years. They are skilled at working with their clients to identify the root cause of an HR problem, they don't overwhelm you with "HR speak," they don't waste your time and they deliver. Throw in a healthy dose of humour and you have the makings of a good team and a great resource book for non-profit organizations both large and small.

The language used in this book is straightforward and clear. The text can be read through and used as a guide and reference as needed. But I must admit to wincing a few times when I read through a few sections of this book. Despite having worked as an Executive Director in the non-profit sector for over twenty years, with nine of those years at the helm of the HR Council for the Non-Profit Sector, I found myself wishing I had managed some HR issues differently or taken more time to do a succession plan or to rethink the design of an organization.

*Even the most seasoned manager will likely learn
something new by reading this book.*

I think we suffer from three important challenges when it comes to effectively managing human resources in our sector. Because we are so focused on our work, running our programs or providing our services, we often don't take the time to set up the structures and processes that will serve us well in the long run. We often start out small and collegial and, before we know it, we have grown to a full staff complement with different people doing different jobs and all having different needs.

Creating the right HR policies, setting up fair and equitable compensation systems, and developing useful performance management programs shouldn't be done on the fly or without regard to good practice; but all too often, we only get to it when a crisis arises. Secondly, we don't know what we don't know. Many managers of nonprofits have come up through the ranks, and love their work and the cause, but they don't necessarily have any training or background in HR management nor do they have the time to acquire those skills. And thirdly, all too often, we suffer from "terminal niceness" in our sector. Terminating employees or addressing poor performance seems antithetical to our values of compassion and help, so we let problems fester until they risk infecting the whole organization. As this book will demonstrate, learning those skills and gaining specific knowledge to address HR challenges can make for a much better night's sleep.

In the non-profit sector, people are at the heart of everything we do. Many of those who come to work in this sector bring with them a solid commitment, if not a passion for the mission of the organization. But nowadays, passion is not enough. We need to attract, support and retain the very best people we can find if we are to achieve real and lasting results, deal effectively with the changes that surround us, learn to innovate, and engage more donors and volunteers to our causes. And that is where effective human resource and organizational management comes into play.

This book will not only help you solve those day to day HR problems; but it makes a real and compelling argument for taking a sustained and strategic approach

The NPO Dilemma: HR and Organizational Challenges
in Non-Profit Organizations

to human resources management and investing in your people. There is nothing more powerful than a well-aligned team of the right people doing the right things at the right time, with a clear focus on results.

Lynne Toupin
Former Executive Director
HR Council for the Non-Profit Sector
Ottawa, Canada

About the Author

Tim McConnell

Tim McConnell is the Managing Partner of McConnell HR Consulting Inc. He is also an Organization Design Consultant with Grahall Partners, LLC.

He is a senior HR Strategist. He has over 25 years experience in Human Resources management, both as a Director of HR and as a senior HR consultant. Tim provides advice and guidance on HR Strategy, Compensation and Organization Design to clients in the public, private and not-for-profit sectors.

Tim holds a Diplôme d'études collégiales (DEC) from Vanier College, a B.A. in Political Science and Economics from McGill University, and a Masters degree in Public Administration from Carleton University. He has earned professional designations in HR in both Canada (CHRP) and the United States (SPHR).

7

He is a Certified Management Consultant (CMC) and recently earned the Human Capital Strategist (HCS) certification from the Human Capital Institute (HCI) in Washington, D.C.

Tim was an adjunct professor in the Advanced Program in HR Management (APHRM) at the Rotman School of Management, University of Toronto from 2002 to 2008. He is also a former sessional lecturer at Carleton University, teaching HR Management in the School of Public Administration from 1993 to 1997.

He is a seasoned public speaker and the published author of several articles on HR management, Succession Planning, Compensation and Organization Design.

Tim is a past-President of the Ottawa Human Resources Professionals Association (OHRPA) and a past-President of the Human Resources Professionals Association of Ontario (HRPAO). He was a member of the Board of Directors of the Boys and Girls Club of Ottawa and Chair of the HR Committee from 2008 to 2011.

He enjoys reading, tennis, winter vacations in Florida, and his summer cottage at Mink Lake near Eganville, Ontario.

McConnell HR Consulting Inc. is a boutique management consulting firm that provides clients in the not-for-profit sector with solutions to strategic HR,

Compensation and Organization Design challenges. The firm was founded in 2002 and has offices in both Ottawa and New York.

Tim McConnell, B.A., MPA, SPHR, CMC, HCS
Senior HR Strategist / Managing Partner
McConnell HR Consulting Inc.
613-836-4648
1-855-836-4648
www.McConnellHRC.com
www.McConnellHRC-NY.com

Warning–Disclaimer

While this book strives to provide the reader with practical guidance and to provide general education on the topic at hand, it is not a substitute for adequate legal or other professional advice. The opinions within represent the opinions of the authors and editors only and, therefore, should not be construed as a position on the part of any particular organization or entity.

Further, nothing herein should be construed as the rendering of legal or other professional advice and the reader is advised to consult with appropriate counsel for obtaining any advice. By reading this publication, no attorney client relationship exists between the reader and either the author or publisher.

1

Introduction

The Non-Profit Sector

There are an estimated 160,000 Non-profit Organizations (NPOs) in Canada, employing 2 million people (11% of the labor force). The sector represents $79.1 billion (Canadian) or 7.8% of the Canadian GDP (larger than the automotive or manufacturing industries).[i] There are over 1.5 million non-profits in the United States.[ii] The non-profit sector is quite large.

NPOs are incorporated organizations which (often) exist for educational or charitable reasons, and from which shareholders or trustees do not benefit financially. Any money earned must be retained by the organization and used for its own expenses, operations, and programs. Many non-profit organizations also seek tax-exempt status and may also be exempt from local taxes.[iii]

It is also a very diverse sector. NPOs (in our firm's definition) include non-governmental organizations (NGOs), para-public agencies, professional associations, lobby groups, foundations, institutes, and charities. NPOs can be found in the arts, cultural, sciences, sports, recreation, religious, financial and social services sectors. A broader definition of NPOs would include hospitals, libraries, museums, colleges and universities.

Some NPOs are large, most are small (with less than 100 staff members), some are well funded, and others struggle for donations. The top 1% of organizations command 60% of all revenues.[iv] Many NPOs exist for a cause; they are mission-driven and exist to achieve a social, political or environmental objective of some type.

What they have in common is not what they are, but what they are not. They are not the government (municipal, provincial / state or federal), nor are they private sector for-profit companies. They are in between. Many Human Resources (HR) policies, practices and procedures found in government and/or the private sector apply to NPOs. Some do not.

Another key differentiator is the type of jobs. NPOs tend to have far more unique (one-employee) positions than private sector companies where many people do the same job. They tend to have far more generalists (people wearing multiple hats) than specialists.

"Nonprofits need specialized expertise. The types of solutions used at multinational, for-profit corporations, can't simply be imposed on mission-driven organizations.

Increasingly, the social sector is faced with complex human resources challenges that require unique responses and solutions. From a continuing national unemployment crisis, to a shortage of qualified human resources professionals with sector specific experience, to the lack of sufficient funding for infrastructure support, many nonprofit organizations are confronted with very real workplace concerns."[v]

Many NPOs are faced with funding shortages, employee turnover, absenteeism, grievances, skill gaps, and stressful work environments. Certainly many are spending more time on their strategic goals today in the areas of fundraising, new technology and client services. The role of Human Resources planning on a strategic level may not be as clearly defined.[vi]

Human Resources

Human Resources management is an interesting profession, to say the least.

Since most people have a job (or had a job), have written a resume, and have been interviewed for a job, they think they are HR experts. This most definitely gives meaning to the old expression "a little bit of knowledge is a dangerous thing," impacting the service delivery capability of HR professionals. Accountants, engineers and rocket scientists generally don't face this problem.

The field of HR also has a problematic reputation. Are HR professionals:

- Those warm and fuzzy, overly nice, "people persons" who spread joy and happiness, parodied in television commercials? Some of the meanest people I have ever met have been Directors of HR – especially in labor relations. My favorite cartoon character is Catbert, the Evil Director of HR.
- Mindless paper pushers?
- The organizational police department? Those pedantic bureaucrats whose goal in life is to dogmatically enforce a myriad of arcane HR rules and regulations?

The seminal article by Fast Company in 2005, "Why We Hate HR," had this to say about the profession:[vii]

- "Strategic HR leadership is an oxymoron. HR people are neither strategic nor leaders."
- "HR is a necessary evil."
- "HR is a dark bureaucratic force that blindly enforces nonsensical rules, resists creativity, and impedes constructive change."
- "HR is a henchman for the CFO."
- "People processes are duplicative and wasteful, creating a forest of paperwork."
- "HR organizations have ghettoized themselves to the brink of obsolescence."
- "HR is uniquely unsuited... to the important role of

raising the reputational and intellectual capital of the company."

- "Most HR managers aren't particularly interested in, or equipped for, doing business."
- "Business acumen is the single biggest factor that HR professionals lack today."
- "HR pursues efficiency in lieu of value."

It isn't just Fast Company. Even the respected *Economist* has weighed in on the subject: "CEOs across the world rated HR as their worst-performing business function. No other function, not even the notoriously unlovable IT-department, came close to being this unappreciated."[viii]

Later that year, the *Globe and Mail* blamed the war in Afghanistan on the HR Department.[ix]

- "War is an HR issue."
- "War is a matter of skilled labor. Guns and planes are of secondary importance."
- "Things (in the war) go wrong due to: hiring, labor shortages, training, specialization, flexibility, size of work force, seniority, re-training, skill set matches, fitting the right people to the right job, and getting the wrong people out of the way."
- "The problem (with the war) is a terrible screw up by the HR department."

To some extent, the pundits have a point:

- We (the HR profession) need to communicate far better to speak the same language as top management to demonstrate how HR practices are linked to business strategy.

- We need to clearly demonstrate HR's value to the organization to prove how "people results" drive the business.
- We need to greatly improve our business acumen to be successful strategic partners, to integrate, and to better understand the business.
- We need to increase our use of HR metrics to link HR practices to organizational performance, to report on performance, and to show the contribution to the bottom line.
- We need to forge a strategic partnership with managers and employees in recognition of the role they play to make the business run.

We actually love HR!

I ♥
HUMAN RESOURCES

HR provides:

- Interesting and challenging work.
- Complex and intellectually demanding issues.
- Challenges to balance the needs of management (and shareholders) with the needs of employees.
- Non-stop problem solving.
- Rewards in finding and engaging talent.

Notwithstanding the quotes above, the press actually has some good things to say about HR:

- HR is the "prime source of sustainable competitive potential." (HR Scorecard, Harvard Business School Press, 2001)
- "Outside of the CEO, HR is the most critical func-

tion of any company." (Jack Welch, *Winning*, Harper Business, 2005)

- "HR Manager Ranks as Fourth Best Job in America." (*Money Magazine*, April 2006)

Deloitte Consulting has written about the evolving role of the Chief HR Officer in organizations.[x] They see Human Resources professionals as being:

- Talent Strategists
  - Contributing to business strategy.
  - Translating business strategy into global workforce requirements.
  - Forecasting talent needs and addressing talent gaps.
  - Orchestrating learning, skills and career development.

- Counselor and Leadership Developers
  - Providing executive coaching for senior leaders.
  - Overseeing leadership development programs.

- Change Masters
  - Building and overseeing change management capacity.
  - Providing change management guidance and services.

- Organizational Architects
  - Providing organization design (OD) and performance optimization consulting.
  - Defining organizational culture and values.
  - Defining a diversity strategy and programs.
  - Designing the workforce environment.

- Performance and Reward Architects
  - Designing and administering performance management and recognition programs.
  - Overseeing and managing compensation and benefits.

- HR Service Delivery Managers
  - Determining the HR service delivery model.
  - Designing and fostering the optimal connection with the company.
  - Managing vendor relationships.
  - Overseeing operational HR activities.
  - Managing HR technology development.
  - Managing HR data, reporting and analytics.

- Regulatory and Risk Managers
  - Formulating and executing HR policies and processes.
  - Managing HR compliance.
  - Managing HR (human capital and workforce) risks.
  - Reporting compliance to management and the Board.

- Corporate Governance Advisors
  - Managing executive succession.
  - Providing Board development and administration services.
  - Supporting the Compensation Committee.

About this Book

This book was written for two reasons.

First: our marketing guys have been advising for years that every good consultant should write a book (or two).

Second (and of far more importance to the reader): our NPO clients regularly face the HR and organizational challenges outlined in this book and have a strong ongoing interest in "what the other guy is doing" – that is, how other NPOs have responded to similar challenges. This is a perspective that a management consultant brings to the table.

Management consultants are like bumble bees, flying from one flower (client) to another cross-pollinating ideas and best practices.

This actual preparation of this book involved four phases.

Phase 1. The first phase was incremental; over the past several years we have written a variety of articles on various HR topics, several of which have been published in trade magazines. We have also prepared a number of PowerPoint slide decks for different seminars and speaking engagements.

Phase 2. The second phase took place during 2011. We assembled and arranged the various articles and slide decks into a logical order, which became the table of contents for this monograph. We then organized the material in each resulting chapter into text that (hopefully) makes sense. My staff assisted in this endeavor. Sincere thanks go out to our Ottawa-based team; Kathy Bedard – Director of HR Consulting, Arron Dobson – HR Consultant, Roslyn Ross – HR Consultant, and Melissa Lanigan – HR Intern.

Phase 3. This phase involved direct research. We validated and corroborated material via the Internet, much of which is referenced in the chapter notes. We made use of direct applications (challenges and solutions) from current client projects. I also interviewed two wonderful people in New York City. Special thanks and appreciation for their time and input go to Mr. Ami Dar, Executive Director of Idealist.org, and Ms. Lynne Plavnick, Vice-President Human Resources at Volunteer America.

Phase 4. This phase was the editing of the overall manuscript, most of which took place in New York City. Being out of town offers tremendous opportunities to escape day-to-day workload pressures and focus one's mind on the task of writing, in between client and partner meetings. The Reading Room at the New York Public Library main branch on Fifth Avenue offered a particularly welcoming oasis of architectural splendor, quiet (hard to come by in downtown Manhattan), Wi-Fi Internet access, and the salutary "osmosis effect" of being surrounded by hundreds of studious minds at work. The library at the Penn Club also offered a pleasant and supportive work environment. The Air Canada departure lounge at La Guardia Airport? Not so much.

The diagram on the front cover is a helix. A helix is a curve in three-dimensional space. We were introduced to helixes and DNA representation while conducting an Organizational Review at Genome Canada. Genome Canada is a not-for-profit organization with a mandate from the Government of Canada to develop and implement a national strategy for supporting large-scale genomics and proteomics research projects.

Our helix represents the three-dimensional complexities of Human Resources management. The two large DNA strands represent management and employees. The interconnecting vertical bars represent the multitude of various HR functions and disciplines (see Chapter 2 – HR Strategy) used to connect management and staff. The bookend on the left is your organization's strategy (both business strategy and HR strategy). The bookend on the right is the desired outcome for your NPO's programs and services – Success!

The NPO Dilemma

A dilemma is a problem offering two possibilities, neither of which is practically acceptable.[xi] The boxes on the front cover illustrate four of the key questions facing NPOs:

- Do you have the right jobs in your organization? There are always choices and tradeoffs to be made here. The answers to which lie in Organization Design (Chapter 3) and HR Strategy (Chapter 2).

- Will the people you hire stay? Are your employees there because they need a job or because they are committed to your cause? (see Chapter 6 – Employee Retention)

- Are you paying properly? Compensation creates several dilemmas for NPOs:

  - What is our market position? Many NPOs are in the social services sector, funded by donations or government grants, and pay far lower than government or the private sector. This position makes it difficult to attract and retain the right skilled staff.
  - A related challenge is when an NPO has a pay policy position for most staff that is at a low level, but finds itself having to pay much higher for specific hot skills such as IT or Development (fundraising).
  - Performance Management and Pay for Performance (merit pay) are also challenges. Do NPOs provide equal annual cost of living adjustments to all staff (like the government)? Or, do they differentiate salary increases based on results-driven performance? How does an NPO quantify results? See Chapter 5 – Compensation for more details.

- Public Sector or Private Sector? Who are NPOs? They are neither the government nor a private company. NPOs tend to have HR policies and practices that are in between these two extremes, yet they often wish to have the best of both worlds.

Other related dilemmas addressed in this book include the CEO vs. COO Dilemma for Executive Directors (Chapter 3 – Organization Design) and the Fairness and Communications Dilemmas (both covered in Chapter 5 – Compensation).

This book is a compilation. It addresses the challenges NPOs face in the main areas of our consulting practice – the ones we work with every day – HR Strategy, Compensation and Organization Design. It also discusses a number of related problematic areas for NPOs, such as Employee Retention and Succession Planning.

Our aim is to provide an overview of the topics addressed in each chapter, to put our own *spin* on the topic in terms of our approach and consulting experiences, and to address some of the unique aspects of HR management in the non-profit sector. We hope and trust the reader will find it useful.

Tim McConnell, MPA, SPHR, CMC, HCS
Managing Partner
McConnell HR Consulting Inc.
Ottawa, Ontario / New York, NY
December 2011

Notes

[i] Imagine Canada (2011)
[ii] National Center for Charitable Statistics (2011)
[iii] www.InvestorWords.com (2011)
[iv] Imagine Canada (2011)
[v] Lisa Brown Morton, President & CEO of Non-Profit Solutions (Washington D.C., 2011)
[vi] Teresa Howe, "Why Do I Need a Human Resources Strategy?" (Charity Village, Toronto, 2002).
[vii] "Why We Hate HR" (Fast Company, 2005).
[viii] The Economist Intelligence Unit, 2006 CEO Survey.

[ix] "What's Gone Wrong in Afghanistan? Blame the HR Department" (*Globe and Mail*, October 28, 2006).

[x] "The Evolving Role of the Chief Human Resources Officer" (Deloitte and Touche LLP, 2005).

[xi] Wikipedia (2011).

2

HR Strategy

What is it, and Why do You Need One?

In the face of significant strategic and operational challenges, most NPOs rely on the skills and competencies of their staff in order to meet business and program objectives.

The goal of this chapter is to help NPOs evolve in developing, evaluating, improving, communicating and applying a winning HR Strategy.

What is It?

First of all, what is a strategy? It's a plan to get you from where you are now to where you want to be in the future.

In fancy terms, "a strategy is a pattern in a stream of decisions – designed to create a specific competitive positioning through deploying organizational resources."[i] It has also been defined as the plans, program, and intentions of developing an organization to meet its present and future competitive challenges in order to generate superior economic value.

An HR strategy is a concrete plan created to direct the development and improvement of HR policies, processes, and approach. It has been further defined by Paul Kearns as "a conscious and explicit attempt to maximize organizational value by gaining a sustainable competitive advantage from human capital."[ii]

The HR strategy identifies the connection between the business of the organization and the employees, and the alignment of the HR function to the organization's primary business strategy.

Why Do You Need One?

You probably don't live in a static world, as much as you'd like to stick your head in the sand and pretend so (at least on some days). It's a turbulent world out there.

The environmental factors hitting NPOs include:

- Globalization.
- The war for talent.
- Increasing pressure on your employees (changing

technology, longer hours, multiple careers, skill changes).
- Continuing decline in employee loyalty.
- Ongoing decline in customer loyalty.
- Interventions of Boards.
- Increased speed of change.

In addition, payroll is the largest budget item in most organizations. You need to spend it wisely.

It is generally accepted that, with equal access to things like funding, equipment, and intellectual property, the organization with the best managed talent will succeed.

An HR strategy is closely linked with:

- More effective HR programs.
- Greater impact of HR on the organization.
- Higher levels of revenue.
- Greater success.

Principles

Strategic HR is based on the following core concepts and principles:

- Talent is the engine behind the creation of all value.
- Every business issue is a symptom of deeper human or organizational issues.
- All business problems are, when you boil them down, HR issues.
- Talent will be the resource of scarcity in the future.
- All HR work must be directly connected to the business strategy and customer needs.

- Line management is responsible for HR work in the organization. Managers manage budgets, technology and people.

What Can You Use an HR Strategy For?

Useful purposes for an HR strategy include:

- Clarifying organizational objectives, goals and priorities.
- Describing a long-term integrated HR plan.
- Ensuring continued alignment with organization's objectives as well as HR policies and procedures.
- Achieving appropriate organization design in relation to the strategic direction of the organization.
- Providing a frame of reference for management and all staff.
- Defining how to best align the skills and competencies of the resources available.

Teresa Howe at Charity Village[iii] advises that the purpose of an HR strategy is to:

- Ensure that the organization has the human capacity and capability to support the organization's goals and objectives.
- Provide effective recruitment, selection, retention and management of the performance of its people.
- Create an appropriate work environment that is in compliance with legislation and is sensitive to both management's and employees' needs.
- Provide structure, compensation, policies, standards, reward systems, benefit programs and grievance handling.
- Foster a culture that reflects organizational values.

The primary objective of strategic HR is to translate business strategies into HR priorities. The deliverable of the HR Strategy is strategy execution: reducing costs, increasing program effectiveness, and increasing revenue.

What Are the Results?

Howe states that good HR management begins by asking the following questions, which correspond to four key results areas:[iv]

- Are people well led? (Leadership)
- Is the organization becoming more productive? (Productive workforce)
- Does the work environment bring out the best in people? (Enabling work environment)
- Do the anticipated needs of the organization match the competencies of its people? (Sustainable workforce)

These four key result areas can be the focus of a healthy, visionary HR strategy.

What Does an HR Strategy Look Like?

Our view of the total scope of an HR strategy looks like this:

HR Strategy Model

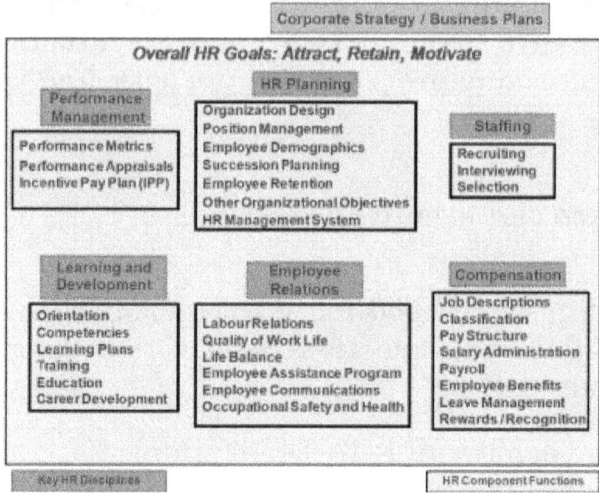

It could also look like this:

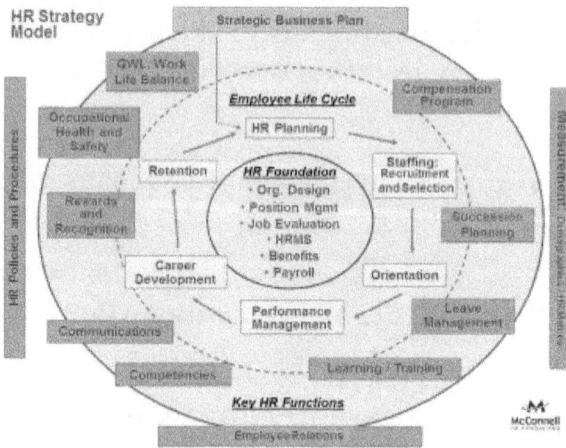

A key point with respect to the above diagrams is that all of the HR disciplines and components are closely related and linked together. They do not exist in isolation. The design and application of any single area will affect, and in turn, be affected by many of the other areas.

Table of Contents

A typical table of contents for an NPO's HR strategy can include the following:

Executive Summary		
1.Introduction	1.1. Background 1.2. HR Issue 1.3. Goals / Objectives 1.4. Benefits	
2. HR Disciplines / Principles	2.1. HR Planning	2.1.1. Organizational Structure 2.1.2. HR Demographics 2.1.2. Capacity Requirements 2.1.4. Work Descriptions 2.1.5. Classification 2.1.6. Succession Planning
	2.2. Recruitment	2.2.1. External Recruitment 2.2.2. Competencies 2.2.3. Internal Resourcing
	2.3. Development	2.3.1. Learning and Professional Development 2.3.2. Career Management 2.3.3. Performance Management

	2.4. Retention	2.4.1. Awards and Recognition 2.4.2. Employee Communications 2.4.3. Quality of Work Life
3. Action Plan	3.1. Priorities / Actions 3.2. Timetable 3.3. Communications	

Advanced HR Strategy

Let's step back a bit and contrast strategic HR with tactical HR.

Tactical HR is the basic administration of people issues and data. It is the implementation of traditional HR programs such as hiring, firing and payroll. In contrast, strategic HR focuses on the link between human talent and winning in the marketplace. It addresses the relationships between human, financial and technological assets in order to build organizational capabilities.

Readers should be able to understand how to conceptualize a desired strategic HR end state, recognize the importance of linking HR Planning to competitive strategy, and know how to create and implement an effective HR strategy within their organization.

The creation and implementation of an effective HR strategy has been closely linked with an increase in the value of HR programs, higher levels of revenue, and greater profitability. Organizations that possess and apply effective HR strategies have shown HR to have a greater impact on the organization as a whole. This in turn has resulted in overall competitive advantage.[v]

Research also shows that with equal access to funding, equipment, and intellectual property, and the firm with the best managed talent will succeed. Developing an HR strategy enables companies to exercise greater control over their budgets and resource allocation, focus more time and attention on strategic value-added activities, utilize HR information systems more effectively, and experience expected return on investments.[vi]

The HR strategy should be the key Human Resource document in the organization, a statement about the strategic role of HR. It should be a concrete plan for the development and improvement of HR policies, processes and approaches. It must define the mission and value of HR and show the way to the future.

The premise of HR value is outlined by Dave Ulrich in *The HR Value Proposition*.[vii] Ulrich argues that in order to provide value to your organization and obtain a competitive advantage, you must develop your HR strategy around the business, not around HR itself. HR's objectives must align with corporate objectives, and HR practices must support the requirements of both internal and external stakeholders. You must have a line of sight to both internal clients (managers and employees) and external clients (the marketplace that your organization serves), and you must align the HR practices with the requirements of both of these stakeholders.

Ulrich advises that organizations assess their business
and market environment and address these questions:

1. What are the organizational capabilities that my
    organization must have to create programs and
    services that produce value for stakeholders?
2. What abilities do our employees need so they can
    understand and respond to stakeholder demands?
3. How do we ensure that our HR professionals know
    what to do and have the skills to do it?
4. How do we identify/invest in HR practices that
    deliver results?
5. How do we organize the HR activities to deliver
    maximum value?
6. How do we create an HR strategy that will help the
    organization succeed?[viii]

If you already have an HR strategy in place, the following is a checklist outlining the core components of an
all-encompassing HR strategy. This checklist will help
determine if your strategy includes all of the necessary
factors.

- Do you have a clear vision and mission that has
  been communicated to all employees?
- Do you have a clear business strategy? If so, what
  are the top three strategic objectives?
- What key HR issues stem from each of the strategic objectives?
- Have you specifically communicated to key staff
  how they have to add value to achieve objectives?
- Do you have clear work principles that every employee understands (such as honest feedback)?

The problem with HR strategies is that there is often
a disconnect between HR's goals and activities and the

overall business strategy. It can be argued that there is no HR agenda per se; the HR strategy must be fully aligned with the objectives of the business strategy, and thus the two are ultimately one and the same.[ix]

Organizations should refrain from separating the HR strategy from the business strategy and stop referring to them as two separate plans. From this perspective, the phrase "integrated business and HR planning" is redundant.

HR Maturity Scale – *Where are you?*

The HR Maturity Scale was developed by Paul Kearns in the U.K.[x] It is a six point scale, ranging from 0 – 5, aimed towards helping an organization determine where they are now (in terms of HR maturity), what the strategic implications of that position are, and what stage they need to reach in order to become a high-value organization.

- Stage 0 – No Personnel Management; represents organizations that have no form of HR management in place and do not adhere to the guidelines of employment legislation.

- Stage 1 – Personnel Administration that puts forth minimal effort to manage and control people costs. The processes consist of hiring, firing, payroll, and basic record keeping.

- Stage 2 – Good Professional Practice represents organizations that may or may not have an HR manager; however, they recognize that professional management practices make a difference and have implemented proper recruitment, selection, and appraisal processes and procedures.

- Stage 3 – Effective HR Management corresponds to firms who make a conscious move towards a systematic and structured approach and have proper recruiting, training, compensation, and performance management programs in place.

- Stage 4 – Integral HR Management. HR management is integral to operations and allows HR to take on the role of a proactive HR Business Partner.

- Stage 5 – Strategic HR Management denotes organizations that have transitioned to advanced systems thinking and high value-added business performance. Stage 5 organizations have an adaptive culture that supports advanced continuous learning.

Most NPOs tend to be somewhere between Stage 2 and Stage 4 on the HR Maturity Scale. Given their very nature, we have never seen, nor would expect to see, an NPO that was at Stage 0. Size is obviously a factor; the larger NPOs generally tend to have HR departments. Many small ones outsource HR (see Chapter 8).

The Girl Scouts of the USA and Volunteer America are two large national NPOs that (in our opinion) have sophisticated HR functions. They have large HR departments, reflect a geographic dispersion, are closely linked to the "raison d'être" of their organizations, and have successfully responded to downsizing issues. They are probably at Stage 4 or 5.

The Business of HR

There are six areas where HR can really add value to the organization. These themes were presented by Mark Withers in his 2010 book, *Transforming HR*.[xi] The themes are:

1. Being at the heart of organizational development.
2. Creating high performance work environments.
3. Designing new organizational architectures.
4. Understanding the workforce and its cost.
5. Using technology to advance knowledge sharing and innovation.
6. Building a compelling employer brand.

Organizational development focuses on the idea of creating and building future organizational capability, defining and shaping organizational strategy and plans, enhancing organizational health, utilizing change management tools and techniques to deliver the strategy, and improving resourcing flexibility.

Creating a high performance work environment enhances an organization's talent management initiatives, develops career paths, enhances proactive redeployment for talent, identifies and addresses leadership development needs, supports ongoing skills development and key position succession planning, strengthens team work and collaboration, and shapes the thinking on finding better ways to reward people.

Understanding the workforce and its costs provides HR with the opportunity to help the business cut costs by optimizing the cost base to do more with less. In order to optimize the cost base, organizations need to evaluate and change cost structures in a way that creates sustainable long-term value and simultaneously delivers cost reductions.

Using technology to advance knowledge sharing and innovation includes the need to be fluent in Web 2.0 social media technologies (such as Facebook, LinkedIn, and Twitter). HR must understand the impact that social media can have on recruiting, corporate branding, orientation, communications, employee engagement, and learning initiatives. Organizations should make advanced technology an inherent part of their HR service delivery model.

Lastly, organizations need to build a compelling employer brand and market the brand as an Employee Value Proposition to not only attract new talent and shape their expectations, but to enhance the psychological contract with existing employees to drive higher levels of engagement and commitment.

Building Your HR Strategy

Two critical questions must be addressed: What kinds of people do you need to manage and run your organization to meet your strategic program and business objectives? What people programs and initiatives must be designed and implemented to attract, develop and retain staff to compete effectively?[xii]

Building an HR strategy involves the following steps:

1. Preparation

- Talk to your management team and program heads.
- Understand your organization: your goals and objectives, programs, business strategy and organization.
- Know the key driving forces in your organization and your environment.
- Understand your workforce requirements (skills needed and capacity).

2. Analysis

- Conduct a SWOT analysis of your organization: Strengths, Weaknesses, Opportunities and Threats.
- Link program and business requirements to HR responsibilities.
- Create an *as-is* view of current HR processes, performance data and the service delivery model.

Ulrich advises knowing your organization and how it functions from a workflow perspective.

- Flow of People – How do people move in, through, up, and out of the organization?
- Flow of Performance Management – What are the standards and measures (qualitative and quantitative), financial and non-financial rewards, and feedback that reflect the accomplishment of stakeholder interest?
- Flow of Information – What keeps people informed within the organization? What is the knowledge, data and information used? How does it flow?

- Flow of Work – What is the work being done? Who does it? How is it done? Where is it done?[xiii]

3. HR Planning

Prepare an HR Plan:

- Forecast your HR needs (based on the data gathered above). Economists call this task Demand Analysis.
- Assess the availability of your current staff. Economists call this task Supply Analysis.
- Conduct a gap analysis, the difference between your availability and your needs.
- Determine net requirements – that is, do you have too many staff and need to lay off, do you have insufficient staff and need to hire, or do you have the right numbers but need to re-train?
- Identify and prioritize the critical people issues facing your organization.
- Create an HR action plan to implement the required actions.

4. Definition

- Define your HR strategy; prepare a strategic model of HR functions.
- For each critical people issue, highlight the options available.
- Determine HR priorities and performance indicators.
- Translate the critical issues, options and priorities into HR component objectives.

5. Finalization

- Validate with key stakeholders and senior leadership.
- Gain approval from the Executive Director / CEO and the Board of Directors.

Our Experience

In our travels we have found that:

Only about half of organizations have an HR strategy. Many say they do, but don't.

Approaches to staff involvement vary significantly:

Some organizations will not involve staff at all or even tell them about the strategy.
Some will have a town hall meeting once a year and proudly present the strategy.
Others will involve staff in extensive interviews, focus groups and workshops in order to maximize participation.

This latter approach is good to a point, but can easily bog down and paralyze the HR strategy development process.

Presenting to the Executive Team

Reaching the executive team is always a challenge. You need to:

- Speak their language.
- Clearly demonstrate good business sense.

- Sell the benefits.
- Tell a story; provide a deliberate narrative flow.
- Provide new insights.
- Visually communicate.
- Present strategic implications, dependencies and outcomes in a visual manner.
- Be knowledgeable. Know your material. Know the business.
- Believe! Be excited.
- Overcome any challenges and obstacles raised.[xiv]

Notes

[i] Henry Mintzberg, *The Rise and Fall of Strategic Planning* (New York: The Free Press, 1993).

[ii] Paul Kearns, *HR Strategy* (Oxford: Butterworth-Heinemann, 2010).

[iii] Teresa Howe, "Why Do I Need a Human Resources Strategy?" (Charity Village, Toronto, 2002).

[iv] Ibid.

[v] Paul Kearns, *HR Strategy* (Oxford: Butterworth-Heinemann, 2010).

[vi] "Setting and Executing HR Strategy" (Corporate Leadership Council, 2004).

[vii] Dave Ulrich and Wayne Brockbank, *The HR Value Proposition* (Boston: Harvard Business Press, 2005).

[viii] Ibid.

[ix] Mark Withers et al., *Transforming HR* (Oxford: Butterworth-Heinemann, 2010).

[x] Paul Kearns, *HR Strategy* (Oxford: Butterworth-Heinemann, 2010).

[xi] Mark Withers et al., *Transforming HR* (Oxford: Butterworth-Heinemann, 2010).

[xii] "Developing an HRM Strategy" (Accel-Team.com, 2008).

[xiii] Dave Ulrich and Wayne Brockbank, *The HR Value Proposition* (Boston: Harvard Business Press, 2005).

[xiv] Luke Wroblewski, "Influencing Strategy by Design: Executive Presentations" (LukeW.com, 2008).

3

Organization Design

Is Your Organization Aligned to Support its Vision and Mission?

Is your organization well designed? How do you know? What does a well designed organization look like, and how does it feel to work there? How is it different from a poorly designed one?[i]

The answers to these questions lie in the functional structure, also known as the organization design, of your work place. You've heard the term before, Organization Design (OD). These two words are familiar to you at a high level, yet may be indistinct as to how they apply to your organization.

Although the concept has been around for ages, many managers are unaware of its strategic impact, and more importantly, how OD should be approached. In this chapter, we will examine the concept of OD and how it can work in your non-profit organization.

Doesn't OD Mean Organization Development?

While they share the same acronym, Organization Design is not to be confused with Organization Development. In fact, these are two separate concepts. Organization Development deals with the "people" side of business performance: leadership, team dynamics, and operational effectiveness.

Organization Development is an effort that is planned, organization wide, and managed from the top. It is intended to increase organization effectiveness and health through planned interventions in the organization's process, using behavioral science knowledge.[ii] It is used to change beliefs, attitudes and values in an organization. Organization Development entails leadership coaching, effective communication strategies, and change awareness, to name a few factors.

The key to recognizing the difference is to understand that Organization Development is a response to Organization Design. In simpler terms, Organization Development deals with "soft" matters, while Organization Design is "hard."

What Do You Mean by Organization?

Put simply, an organization is a group of people who work together with a purpose, mission and vision. It is also viewed as a social arrangement: one which pursues collective goals, controls its own performance, and has a boundary separating it from its environment.

An organization is a dynamic and open social system, which:

- Interacts with its environment.
- Draws input from external sources.
- Transforms inputs into outputs.

Every organization has six components:

1. Purpose / mission / vision
2. Work / tasks
3. Individuals / groups
4. Core work processes
5. Supporting processes
6. Culture

Let's briefly examine each of these components:

1.   Purpose / Mission / Vision

The most core component of any organization is its purpose. Organizations exist to move a business or program goal forward. Businesses organize themselves in a way that will increase their capacity to fulfill their contract with their customer or stakeholder.

An organization can be a loose entity. For example, a business does not have to have an organization. A woman wants to be a professional skater. Her organization will consist of herself, her manager, and her coach in addition to her equipment supplier, insurance agent, lawyer, travel agent, costumer, and stylist.

2.   Work / Tasks

The work component is what people do in the organization. Work is comprised of tasks and duties. A task is a piece of work assigned or done as part of one's duties. It may be an activity that needs to be accomplished repeatedly or sometimes within a defined period of time. It is only for the goal of doing work, or accomplishing an activity; it is there as a need for people to come together to form an organization.

3.   Individuals / Groups

People are organized into groups according to how the work flows though the organization. These groups are often assembled into structures: such as units, branches, or departments. However, the structure of the group does not necessarily equal the design of the organization.

4.   Core Work Processes

Work processes indicate how the work is done. They are procedures or courses of action intended to achieve a result. A business process is a collection of related, structured activities or tasks that produce a specific service or product. Core work processes are those that are sanctioned by the organization – written down, trained on, measured on – and are considered key for achieving the group's work.

5.   Supporting Processes

A supporting or enabling process is one that exists inside the organization to help achieve the work, but which may not be a process officially sanctioned by the organization. It also may be considered non-critical in achieving the group's work. An example of a supporting process is one which recognizes a special accomplishment within a group.

6.   Culture

Culture is defined as the deeply rooted beliefs, values, and norms shared by the members of an organization. It is the personality of an organization, reflected in how employees think, act and feel, as well as how they dress and how they answer the phone. Although these beliefs and values are not directly visible, they drive culture and are reflected in the actions taken by an organization, often characterized by the phrase "it's the way we do things around here."

Definitive and separate groups with an organization can be sub-cultures in themselves: such as, HR vs. faculty vs. public works groups within a university. A quick way to assess your culture is to answer the following questions:

- What ten words would you use to describe your organization?
- Around here, what is really important?
- Around here, who gets promoted?
- Around here, what behaviors get rewarded?
- Around here, who fits in and who doesn't?

The answers to these questions will vary significantly from one culture or sub-culture to another.

In our world of HR consulting, a student intern once observed that we (the HR consultants) spoke and acted differently when meeting and interacting with HR managers than we did when meeting with line managers from other departments in a client organization. We did not realize we were doing it! Upon reflection, we agreed that, yes, we unconsciously lapsed in lingo, shorthand, and certain attitudes when meeting with fellow tribe members.

So What Exactly is Organization Design?

Let's look at a few definitions. Organization Design is used to match the form of the organization as closely as possible to the purposes the organization seeks to achieve. It is about determining the configuration of formal organizational arrangements including the formal structures, processes and systems that make up an organization. It is also:

- About how work gets done. It examines the link between the goals of the organization and how managers and staff are working to achieve those objectives.[iii]

- A process for improving the probability that an organization will be successful by assessing and re-shaping structure and positions to better meet (business) goals. It is a formal, guided process for integrating the people, information and technology of an organization.
- Used to match the *form* of the organization as closely as possible to the purpose(s) the organization seeks to achieve.[iv]
- About determining the configuration of formal organizational arrangements, including the formal structures, processes and systems that make up an organization.[v]
- The way an organization is structured to comply with a strategic plan.

Organization Design deals with the allocation of tasks, reporting relationships and levels to provide a means of achieving full organizational alignment between the "people" aspects and the function. This alignment refers to the complete integration of skills, jobs and people with the goals, functions and structure of the environment on an ongoing basis.

Is This a Good Thing?

An effective organizational design helps communications, increases productivity and fosters innovation. It creates an environment where people can work effectively.[vi]

According to Capelle Associates Inc. (an Organization Design consulting firm in Toronto and Montreal), the benefits include:

- Increased employee output.
- Improved employee satisfaction.
- Improved customer and stakeholder satisfaction.
- Increased growth in services.
- Improved financial performance.
- Improved competitive advantage.
- Significant return on investment.[vii]

When Should We Re-Design?

In their book, *Competing by Design*, Nadler and Tushman[viii] advise that a significant redesign is called for when your organization evolves to the point at which there are substantial congruence problems between the formal organizational arrangements and the other components of your business (such as reporting, business processes, information, performance measurement and control systems). These situations may be driven by:

- Strategic shifts (in competition, regulation, technologies, markets or resources) resulting in a re-definition of work requirements.
- Cultural or political change.
- Growth.
- Staffing changes (such as new leadership, or changes in needs, preferences or skill levels).[ix]

Warning signs and symptoms of ineffective organization design to watch for include:

- Lack of inter-office coordination.
- Excessive friction and conflict among internal groups.

- Unclear roles.
- Under-utilized and/or misused resources.
- Poor work flow.
- Reduced responsiveness to change.
- The existence of silos that block intra-organizational coordination.
- Decreased financial performance.
- High employee dissatisfaction and turnover.
- Proliferation of extra organizational units, such as task forces, committees and projects.[x]

Another warning sign and symptom of inadequate Organization Design is "multiple boss syndrome,"[xi] where staff have more than one reporting relationship and are pulled in different directions by competing priorities. This syndrome often results from the lack of clear managerial and cross-functional accountabilities and authorities.

Our firm's experience has shown that NPOs often require an organizational redesign as a result of:

- Organic growth – the organization has grown one position or one unit at a time in an unplanned fashion.
- External impacts – such as mergers or amalgamation.
- Changes in technology – such as the introduction of a new ERP (Enterprise Resource Planning) computer system.
- Changes in business requirements – such as a new program or service offering.
- Changes in leadership – where the current structure does not support the goals of new management.

So Why Doesn't Everybody Do This?

- They are hanging onto shreds of hope that the problem will fix itself.
- Internal politics prevent them.
- They don't know how it got to be so bad in the first place.
- They believe the problem is not with the organization, but with the marketplace.
- Certain executives have pet strategies that they don't want to give up.
- It's scary to jumble up all that is comfortable. As the saying goes, " The devil you know is better than the devil you don't know."
- Competing priorities exist.
- "We're NOT ready!"

What Does the Design Model Look Like?

Organization Design is much more than simply your structure or your organization chart. It is the process of aligning your organization's structure with its mission (see the following illustration.) It means looking at the complex relationships between tasks, workflow, responsibility and authority – and making sure these all support the objectives of the business.[xii]

As illustrated in the following, there is a direct link (or at least there should be) from operations and business plans all the way to your corporate strategy, mission and vision.

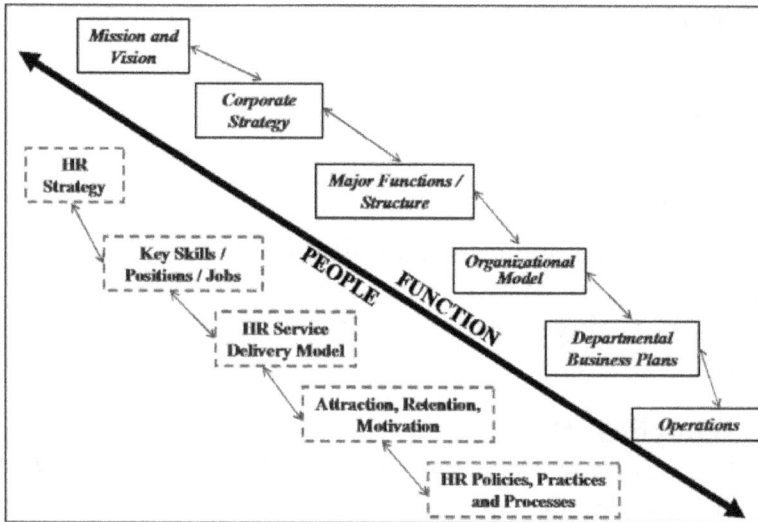

When change takes place, the functions, roles, responsibilities and skills of jobs and positions change. This automatically impacts the entire HR discipline (HR planning, recruitment, resourcing, training and learning, performance management, classification, employee relations, and compensation) and must be fully supported by an effective HR strategy and HR service delivery model.

What Are the Key Concepts in Organization Design?

These include:

1. Business models
2. Design criteria
3. Organizational dimensions
4. Types of organization structures
5. Structural considerations

Let's briefly examine each of these concepts:

1. Business Models

A model is anything used in any way to represent anything else. A conceptual business model portrays the major activities of the organization and the groups of people that play a role in running it. It answers the questions:

- What does the organization do? (business functions)
- Who does it? (the key organizational units)
- Where do they do it? (location)
- What information is needed to support the business?

The diagram that follows is a generic example of a conceptual business model.

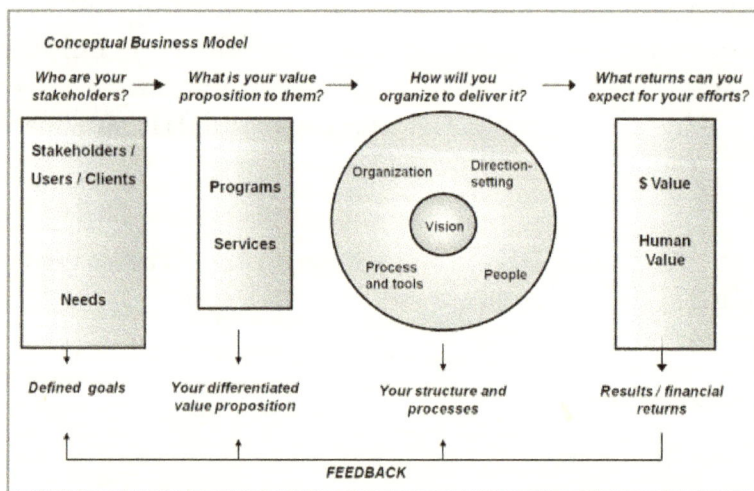

Conceptual Business Model

Our Executive Director clients love these models. They find them quite useful. The models provide a 50,000-foot view of the organization, objectives, core programs and processes, and results / outputs. One CEO liked his model so much he had it printed in color on a heavy stock and carried it with him to meetings with executives, employees, stakeholders, clients and Board Directors. He liked to hold it up and say, "This is what we do."

You may wish to prepare a conceptual business model for your own non-profit organization. Some key questions to ask in order to prepare this are:

- Who are your stakeholders?
- Who are the recipients, end users, and clients of your programs and services?
- What value do you provide to them?
- What needs do you fill?
- What programs and services do you offer them?
- What sector or market segments do you serve?
- With which other nonprofits do you share these stakeholders and sectors?
- How are you organized to deliver your programs and services?

2. Design Criteria

Design criteria (sometimes called specifications) are a useful thinking and communication tool. Essentially, they list all the things that the organization needs to feature to satisfy stakeholders and clients. Design criteria are like the bullet points on the side of a product's package – a list of the key benefits offered.

They are the quality requirements of the organization design, a checklist of the end states, goals or outcomes that the organization wishes to accomplish. Design criteria should be established early in the design process with critical stakeholders. They are used to test emerging assumptions, suggestions, data analyses, and design alternatives, and to test alternative design solutions against key problems.

The following table provides some examples of generic design criteria:

The criterion ...	Means that the selected design ...
Form Follows Function	Meets the purpose for which it was intended or the expressed vision and mission of the organization
Environmental Fit	Meets the requirements of the situation or the demands of the relevant organization environment
Strategic Capability	Protects, enhances or leverages key capabilities of the organization in developing value for customers
Efficiency	Enhances knowledge, communication, feedback, security, and the general quality of work processes
Availability	Makes appropriate and creative use of available resources and technology in product/service and process design
Meaningfulness	Honors the contribution of the past/current culture yet focuses on needed changes in the future culture
Job-Person Fit	Matches the psychological needs of people with the task demands of the organization
Feasibility	Is capable of being implemented within cost and resource constraints
Alignment & Congruence	Enables the relevant parts and aspects of the organization to reinforce, support and work well together in meeting business challenges

Design criteria can also include efficiency, effectiveness, high quality services and programs, fast turnaround, flexibility, and broadening employee skills.

3. Organizational Dimensions

Things to consider include:

- Division of labor (departmentalization and/or specialization).
- Departmentation (functional, purpose and/or location-based).
- Coordination and control (chain of command, span of control).
- Authority and responsibility.
- Line activities versus staff activities.
- Job design.[xiii]

4. Types of Organization Structures

There are four major types of organization structures: functional, program/service based, matrix, and process based.

A. Functional Structure. In this type of structure, activities are grouped by a common function from the bottom to the top of the organization. All people performing the same function are grouped together. Aspects to consider include:

- Hierarchical structure.
- Pyramid structure.
- Units: for example, Marketing, Finance, Operations, Engineering, Employee Services.

- Specialists working together.
- Similar resources are centralized.
- Management is well versed in area of specialization.
- Career paths are defined along specialty.
- The focus is on the area of specialty instead of on overall goals.
- Coordination across areas is difficult.

Most of the NPOs we work with use a traditional functional structure such as: Programs, Member Services, Conference, Marketing / Communications, Finance and Accounting, and IT.

B. Program or Service-Based Structure. This structure is unique in that the grouping – by individual services, major projects or programs, divisions or business centers – is always based on organizational outputs. Programs and / or services which are similar are the organizing element here. Aspects to consider include:

- Resources may be available from other parts of the larger organization
- Resources may not be used as efficiently as possible throughout the organization
- Management is familiar with all areas of the work
- The focus is on programs / services delivered
- Coordination across functions within program / service area is simplified
- Coordination with other program / service areas may be more complex

We have seen this latter point illustrated within an international aid agency. The organization consisted of two major departments: International Programs (who liaised with, arranged, and provided food donations and support to in-country agencies overseas) and Finance (who kept track of all the money – donors, commitments, payables, taxes and reports). Within themselves, each department functioned beautifully. Serious issues arose when they had to interact with each other; they had different skill sets, work processes and values.

The straight-laced "suits" in Finance couldn't understand how the expats in Programs couldn't fill out the right forms on time. The Program folks couldn't understand how the "suits" didn't see that it was not about paperwork, it was about helping starving children.

C. Matrix Structure. This structure overlays two organizational forms in order to leverage the benefits of both. For example, the HR Manager in a geographic region may report to both the Regional Director in the field and the corporate Director of HR in head office. Features of this structure include:

- A combination of function and program/service structures
- Individuals and work units report to a function head and a program/service head
- Reporting relationships and responsibilities are complex
- Individuals typically develop strong identification with one work area/manager

- Coordination across functions and program/service areas is easier
- Management is well versed in their own area and familiar with all areas of work
- It develops individuals who can perform as general managers
- It increases communication throughout the organization

D. Process-Based Structure. This structure is driven by the way the organization organizes around the various streams of work that must get done and not around the functions, locations, or programs. Examples include a payroll process, a snow removal process, and a program development process.

- Teams are organized around critical workflow processes.
- The structure is determined by the outputs and inputs of the process.
- The overall structure has both core and support processes.
- Process Leaders manage a variety of teams engaged in creating similar outputs.
- The focus is on ensuring the processes are aligned and can deliver on the requirements of the next process.
- It helps ensure that the hand-offs between one work group and the next are as smooth as possible.

5. Other Structural Considerations

These include:

- **Flat Organizations (few management levels)**

  - Response time to clients / stakeholders can be faster due to faster internal decision making.
  - Employees feel more in touch with the thinking of top management.
  - Less management support for employees, more self-sufficient.
  - Fewer opportunities for promotion.

A challenge for many Executive Directors of small to mid-sized NPOs is something we call the CEO / COO Dilemma. The Executive Director is called upon to play two distinct roles: Chief Executive Officer – with an upward, external perspective, and Chief Operating Officer – with a downward, internal perspective. In any given week, it may be a challenge for the Executive Director to be flying across the country giving speeches or attending meetings with Board members and key clients / stakeholders, while at the same time being in the office directing and managing day-to-day operations.

Those NPOs with the right size and funding levels can easily split the job in two and have both a CEO and a COO. Others survive by either minimizing the CEO-type activities and / or by having a strong team of Directors in house to "manage the store." This latter structure requires department Directors who are very qualified in their own disciplines and who can also interact as an effective team ("play well") with the other Directors.

- Tall Organizations (numerous management levels)

  - Communication tends to be slower and less accurate because information goes through more people.
  - Decisions tend to take longer; requires coordination across functional boundaries.
  - Employees feel less in touch with the thinking of top management.
  - Supervisory load is less for each manager; opportunity for closer work supervision.
  - More opportunities for promotion.

- Span of Control, including:

  Narrow Span of Control

  - Appropriate in cases where work to be supervised is complex and unpredictable, requires close coordination, employees are unskilled or inexperienced, and the manager is expected to perform other work in addition to supervision.
  - Cost of management is greater.
  - Each manager has more time to manage.
  - Employees have the opportunity for more individual attention and support.

  Broad Span of Control

  - Appropriate where the work is straightforward, standard procedures exist to guide work, employees are highly capable, experienced and self-motivated/self-directed, other sources of support/expertise are available, and work groups are more autonomous.
  - Costs of management are lower.

- Supervisory task is more difficult because management time is spread more thinly.
- Employees exercise more independent judgment, broader levels of skill.

We Have a New Strategic Direction, How Do I Approach Organization Design to Ensure Our New Goals Can be Achieved?

There are six key elements involved in reviewing the current structure for effective Organization Design.

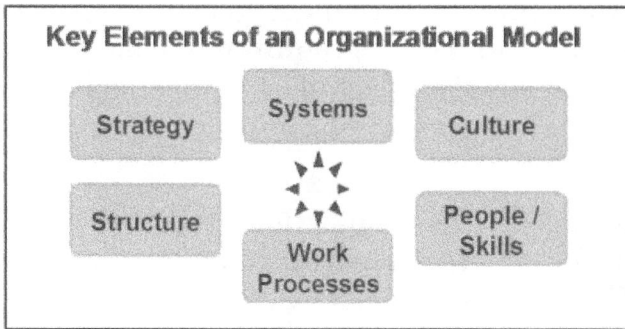

Key Elements of an Organizational Model

Strategy • Systems • Culture • Structure • Work Processes • People / Skills

The best way to re-structure the organization and produce effective results is to base your design on the overall *strategy* and goals of the business. Use the vision, mission, and strategic plan of your organization as a reference point and guide to where the change will take you. The *strategy* element of Organization Design answers the question, "What goal are we trying to accomplish?" Without understanding the link to the strategy component, your new structure will be ineffective, to say the least.

Once the goals and strategy are determined, current functions, work processes and interconnected activities need to be identified and assessed. What is it that you do? What are the major functions of your business? Do the current work units and reporting relationships support the strategic plan? An in-depth understanding of current processes is vital to understanding what needs to be changed.

Now that you have assessed functions and work processes, the organizational structure component needs to be addressed. Do we need to add a new work unit? Should we combine portions of work units? How many levels of management are required to meet the strategic plan? Would a matrix design be more effective in reaching our goals?

The answers to these questions will lead you to begin thinking about designing your new organizational chart. Hold on...not so fast! Before you start to put pen to paper and move boxes around, there are more factors that need to be considered. The actual work systems need to be acknowledged. What is the business plan for each unit? Who is monitoring the work? How are resource allocation and technology implemented? How do the support functions contribute?

At this point in the process, you have reviewed your strategic plan, work processes, structure, and systems. For all of these factors to be effective, they need to be executed by the best employees with carefully planned roles and responsibilities. This task involves integrating people, professions, and skills. Will you hire a new manager from outside or promote from within? Do the existing employees have the skills required to fulfill new responsibilities as a result of required changes?

This can be accomplished through a "staff mapping" exercise which maps employees and skills to positions and highlights variances.

CASE STUDY
Top Seven Warning Signs of Poor Organization Design in the ABC Agency

Do these symptoms exist in your office? Let's examine the case of the ABC Agency (name protected).

1. Silos - Lack of Inter-Office Coordination

An international aid agency had a mandate to deliver health programs for children in Less Developed Countries. They had two departments and two types of staff: the accountants who collected, processed, and reported on funds from donors; and the scientists who designed and administered programs. The accountants were frustrated because the scientists didn't fill out the right financial forms on time. The scientists were mad at the accountants because "it's not about the money, it's about the children." There was a clear lack of communication. The Executive Director was under pressure from the Board to track funding commitments accurately and show positive program results.

2. Excessive Internal Friction and Conflict

*The environment was characterized by excessive
friction and conflict. "Internecine warfare" was the
term we used, as it was harmful and destructive to
both sides involved. Nasty emails abounded, financial reports were late, committed funds were left sitting in back accounts, supplies for field programs
were not delivered, and donors were threatening to
walk.*

3. Lack of a Common Vision

*The agency was characterized by the lack of a broad-
er vision and role perspective by staff. The accountants' job description specified their role – to collect,
process, and report on funds. They diligently pur-
sued their financial goals, but had never visited a
field site. The scientists had a minimal awareness
of where the funding came from. As long as their
supplies arrived on time, they were happy. There
was a lack of common goals between departments.*

4. Unclear Roles and Reporting

*The agency also lacked more specific role defini-
tions, especially on the Program side. The field
scientists in head office reported to the Director of
Programs. The field scientists in Africa reported to*

the Regional Director for Africa. Global programs were created by the Director of Partnerships. Contracts for supplies were managed by the Director of Contracting. The Director of IT oversaw the use of all technology. Territorial disputes were rampant. Staff suffered from multiple boss syndrome.

5. Misused and Under-Utilized Resources

In head office, the monthly and annual work cycles varied. The accountants were busy at the end of every month chasing down missing forms and preparing their reports. They sat around mid-month with nothing to do. The scientists were busy at the start and middle of each month liaising with the field managers and suppliers. Once all the supplies were delivered, they sat around at the end of each month with nothing to do.

6. Poor Work Flow

The overall function of the agency involved finding donors, obtaining funding, developing programs, matching funds to programs, arranging contracts, purchasing and delivering supplies, monitoring results, and reporting to donors. The Executive Director's favorite expression was "Where is my money?" because multiple staff were involved in these functions and the status of funds could not be tracked on a daily basis from donor to delivery.

7. High Employee Dissatisfaction and Turnover

*Even the brightest employees were prevented
from doing their best work and became frustrated because the organization was poorly designed.
Recruiting and training costs soared.*

*What happened to the agency? They re-organized.
They adopted a bicameral functional structure with
the Executive Director and two Directors. The Director
of Corporate Services was responsible for Accounting,
IT and Contracting. All scientists and field programs
report to the Director of Programs. The directors meet
daily. Roles and processes were revitalized. The Executive Director was freed up to act as CEO, be more
strategic, and manage Board, partner, and donor relationships. Twice a year he visits the field and delivers
a slide presentation about accomplishments in a staff
town hall.*

*A year later the ABC Agency became a major grant
recipient in the Global Health Program of the Bill and
Melinda Gates Foundation.*

Notes

[i] "Organization Design: Aligning Organizational Structure with
Business Goals" (MindTools.com, 1995).
[ii] Rickey W. Griffin, *Management, 8th edition*. (Illinois: Houghton
Mifflin, 2005), 13.
[iii] "What is Organization Design?" (Capelle Associates Inc.,
Toronto, 2006).

[iv] Roy H. Autry, "What is Organization Design?" (Inovus, Atlanta, 1996).

[v] David A. Nadler and Michael L. Tushman, *Competing by Design* (New York: Oxford University Press, 1997).

[vi] MindTools.com (1995).

[vii] Capelle Associates Inc., "What is Organization Design?"

[viii] Nadler and Tushman, *Competing by Design*.

[ix] Nadler and Tushman, *Competing by Design,* and Capelle Associates Inc., "What is Organization Design?"

[x] Nadler and Tushman, *Competing by Design*.

[xi] "Multiple Boss Syndrome." (Capelle Associates Inc., Toronto, 2009).

[xii] MindTools.com (1995).

[xiii] Dr. Chun Wei Choo, Faculty of Information Studies, University of Toronto (2007).

.

4

Staffing

Who's on First?

Unless you are running an automated factory staffed with robots, your NPO needs people (also referred to by our clients as human resources, employees, staff, FTEs, the help, a pair of hands, and warm bodies).

You need people to operate, direct and manage your non-profit organization. You need people to answer the phone (although that is often automated), to design your programs, to provide your services, and to communicate with your members and stakeholders.

The trick is finding the people and making sure they are the right people. The question is who are the right people and how do you get them on board?

Our Experience

The approach to staffing varies extensively across NPOs. Some organizations are quite stable and only need to recruit on a periodic replacement basis. When they do, they make use of proper HR Planning to carefully re-validate the need for the position and its duties and qualifications.

NPOs in the Social Services sector often face high turn-over. Front-line social services roles require a specific population with unique skills, a belief in making a difference, and a tolerance for low pay.

At the other end of the spectrum are the roller coaster NPOs. These organizations do minimal HR Planning and hire to fill immediate needs, usually in a hurry. They won't hesitate to lay off or terminate employees whenever the function is no longer needed. They often re-hire for the same job a few months later.

Needless to say, the second group spends far more money on staffing, training and outplacement expenses.

In this chapter, we will explore the recruitment and selection process and how you can ensure you're hiring the right people to make your NPO a success.

Recruitment – What is It?

Recruitment is the ongoing process of attracting people to the organization and encouraging qualified individuals to apply. An effective recruitment process ensures that an organization has the right people, in the right place, at the right time.

We all know that inadequate recruitment can result in retention issues, the inability to attract top talent, and a decrease in an organization's overall program and financial success. This decrease is often a direct result of the high costs associated with hiring an unqualified or poor fit candidate. Associated costs can include expenses related to training, orientation, poor performance, termination, resignation, and expenses a company will incur in rehiring and retraining another employee to fill the vacancy.

It is important that you invest the time and effort to ensure that you are hiring the right person for the job and are not just trying to fill a void in a hurry.

Why is It Important?

In the past (by that I mean the Baby Boomer past), people thought that jobs were hard to find, so when offered a standard position, most people took it. However, in recent years finding the right person for your organization is challenging, especially now that people want more from their employment offers.

Hiring the wrong employee is costly, time-consuming, and can be detrimental to your organization's work environment. On the other hand, hiring the right employee can result in an increase in productivity, high employee morale, a motivated workforce, a competitive advantage, and the skill sets required to move your organization forward. The quality of your organization's workforce initially depends on how well you recruit and select employees. It is an effective way to diversify your organization by bringing in new knowledge, skills, experiences, and abilities, and grow your organization.

A well-planned recruitment process can:

- Reduce labor turnover by hiring candidates that are properly matched to the job and the organization. Employees often leave an organization because the job does not meet their expectations. A solid recruiting process will provide candidates with a realistic job preview that allows the opportunity to ensure their values, expectations, and motivations are aligned with those of the organization.
- Increase the quality and diversity of the candidate pool by advertising clear, concise and appealing job postings through sources that target ideal candidates.
- Attract top talent by effectively branding your organization and establishing relationships with the labor market using social media.
- Enhance a competitive advantage by hiring and retaining top talent.

The Recruitment Process

The recruitment process (as distinct from the Selection process addressed below) can be broken down into four steps:

1. Identify the vacancy.
2. Prepare the job description.
3. Create the job posting.
4. Advertise the job posting.

1. Identify the Vacancy

The first step in the recruitment process is to determine the need for a new or replacement position. If it is a new position, you should consider (in an ideal world) why there is a need. What skills are required to be successful in this position? Does the position need someone part-time or full-time? Is this a temporary or permanent position? Always ensure that you are obtaining the necessary approvals to move forward with staffing the role before wasting any time and energy on starting the hiring process.

2. Prepare the Job Description

In creating the job description, you will be able to develop and prioritize the key requirements needed from the position. If the position already exists, then ensure you are taking the time to update the job description to ensure that it reflects the needs of the role moving forward. Do not get stuck in the trap of "this position was always responsible for..." or "that task never used to be a part of this job..." Now is the time to re-create the position and to find the candidate that will best meet your needs now and moving forward.

In creating the job description, you may also become aware of any constraints that may have an impact on the recruiting process (such as any specialized skills that are required or whether the appropriate candidates are in high demand or low supply). It is important that you take note of these constraints and begin brainstorming how you can overcome them to ensure a successful recruitment process.

3. Create the Job Posting

Your job posting should be based on the job description and identified constraints. The job posting is the tool that will allow you to attract the ideal candidates by providing all the necessary information to the labor pool.

Information to incorporate into the job posting includes:

- Brief overview of the company, its culture, and what it has to offer. This will answer the key question "Why would I want to work here?"
- Title of the vacant position
- Summary of the main duties and responsibilities
- Necessary qualifications, skills, or experience
- Behavioral and technical competencies required
- Benefits associated with the position and the organization
- Instructions on how to apply

- The deadline for the application
- Company contact information

4. Advertising the Job Posting

Last, but not least, you must advertise your job posting. Advertising can often be tricky for nonprofits, as many NPOs do not have the financial means to advertise in multiple places, and it can get costly quickly!

Internal recruitment can be a cost-effective method and has the additional benefit of leading to increased employee morale. Internal sources include:

- Skills inventory
- Nominations
- Employee referrals
- In-house temporary pools
- Replacement and succession plans
- Intranet recruitment ads

However, keep in mind that internal recruitment can also restrict the inflow of new ideas and a fresh perspective.

We know an NPO who offers the best jobs, pay and work environment in their (health-related) sector. New employees come from hospital and/or shift work into a 9 to 4 job in a plush office. Their biggest HR challenge? Zero turnover. Nobody wants to leave. This inhibits the organization's ability to "bring in fresh blood" and to offer internal mobility and career growth opportunities to staff.

External recruitment, although more costly, allows you to draw from a larger labor market, hire employees with new knowledge, skills, and abilities, and recruit for diversity. External sources include:

- Former employees
- Unsolicited applicants
- Online recruitment ads
- Educational institutions
- Employment agencies
- Professional associations
- Print media
- Specialized magazines
- Job fairs
- Social media
- Employment sites

The recruitment process can be implemented in the traditional passive method or using a more proactive approach by using social media to search for the appropriate applicants instead of posting an advertisement and waiting for them to find you.

Market, Market, and Then Market Some More!

Recruiting is all about marketing. If you want to attract top talent, you first need to appeal to top talent. To be a good recruiter you must be able to successfully market your organization to the talent pool. You need to find a way to showcase your organization in a way that will entice top talent to apply.

A for-profit company, ComDev – an aerospace engineering firm, runs ads with two unique eye-catching headings. One reads "This is rocket science," and the other says "The sky is not the limit."

A way to attract talent to the organization, instead of having to search for talent, is to become an employer of choice (see the following section on Employee Value Propositions). This means that the employer values its employees and, in return, employees choose to work there, which results in lower turnover.

In today's world, marketing in terms of recruitment requires much more than posting a job ad in the classified section of the newspaper. Organizations now have the means to get in front of the right people at the right time as opposed to waiting and hoping that the right person will find them. The internet and social media have changed the way in which we reach out to potential applicants. You now have the opportunity to target your job ad to a unique skill set.

Through the use of Web 2.0, organizations can now interact with the labor market and develop relationships with potential applicants. However, it should be pointed out that engaging in social media means more than simply opening an account; to be effective you must be active. Social media is a way for you to communicate the values of your organization to the public, build brand awareness, and provide realistic job previews to future applicants. Social media tools can include, but are not limited to, blogs, social networking sites (Twitter, LinkedIn, Facebook), e-newsletters, videos, and corporate career sites.

Employee Value Proposition

You also require an Employee Value Proposition (also called an Employer Value Proposition or EVP). This is a term used to denote the balance of the rewards and benefits that are received by employees in return for their performance in the workplace.[i] It is closely related to the concept of employer branding.

An EVP is defined as a set of associations and offerings provided by an organization in return for the skills, capabilities and experiences an employee brings to the organization. The EVP is an employee-centered approach aligned to existing, integrated workforce planning strategies because existing employees and the external target audience have validated it. An EVP must be unique, relevant and compelling if it is to act as a key driver of talent attraction, engagement and retention.[ii]

The Selection Process

Once you have completed the final stage of the recruitment process you are halfway there! Unlike the recruitment process, which tries to create a large pool of qualified applicants, the selection process tries to narrow the pool of candidates, leaving you with a few top applicants who possess the pre-determined qualifications to make them a successful candidate. Well developed assessment tools for screening, interviewing, reference checking and more can help you make an informed candidate selection.

The following five steps will help you to narrow down the initial applicant pool and identify the candidate that is right for the job and has the potential to contribute to your organization's goals and objectives.

1. Pre-screening
2. Selection interviews
3. Post-interview assessment
4. Reference checks
5. Hiring decision

1. Pre-Screening

Pre-screening job applicants allows employers to narrow down the pool of applicants to those who are the best fit for the position – without spending hours doing in-depth interviews. Anyone can look good on paper, but a thorough pre-screening can separate the most appropriate applicants from all the rest and enables employers to save the lengthy interview process for only the very best.[iii]

BCJobs offers the following advice:

Methods of Pre-Screening Job Applicants

- *Cover letter:* The applicant's cover letter should be a concise and well-crafted overview of their most relevant work experience for the job. It should neatly summarize why the candidate is well qualified for the position; it should be free of errors and easy to read. Poorly constructed cover letters are generally considered grounds to eliminate a potential candidate.

- *Resume:* The applicant's resume should reflect the skills and experience listed in the job posting. Look for keywords that match the qualities you are seeking. Be attuned to potential red flags such as long gaps in employment and spelling errors. Ensure the candidate's educational background is in line with the position. Look for a well-organized resume that has been customized to the specific position.

- *Phone interview:* You may wish to interact briefly with potential candidates by phone in order to get a better idea of their ability to present themselves verbally. Select a few key questions, no more than five, and keep the conversation brief. Take notes so that you can compare candidate responses later. Be sure to evaluate both the quality of the responses, as well as the candidate's understanding of, and enthusiasm for, the position.

What to Look for When Pre-Screening Job Applicants

What you look for when pre-screening applicants depends on the hard skills an applicant will need to do the job. However, there are other additional factors you will want to consider that may make or break an applicant's chances of getting a full interview. These include:

- *Salary expectations: Some employers ask for salary expectations immediately in order to ensure the candidate's expectations are in line with the budget.*

- *Personal attributes: Characteristics like work ethic, integrity and personal values go a long way toward setting candidates apart – and ensuring the best fit with your organization's work culture.*

- *Soft skills: The ability to communicate clearly, to work well with others, and to problem solve are examples of soft skills that don't necessarily come across effectively on a resume. However, a pre-screening assessment or interview can identify whether a candidate's skills in these and other critical areas match the job requirements.*

A well-conducted pre-screening process should give an employer a solid list of applicants to interview more thoroughly, and some initial insight into those applicants, allowing the full interview to probe more deeply into each applicant's most relevant skills and experience.[iv]

Here is a sample Pre-Screening Form we prepared in the hiring process for an NPO Project Officer.

Sample Pre-Screening Form for NPO Project Officer										
Name	Pre-Screening Criteria					Ranking			Comment	Forward Resume to Client
	University Degree	Current Role / Employer	Experience in a Professional NPO Environment	Experience in Project Mgmt	Experience With Project Mgmt Tools	A	B	C		
A	Masters of Education	Project Coordinator - Education Department of NPO	No	Yes	Yes	A			Experience with developing online resources and maintaining programs.	Yes
B	Masters of Philosophy in Policy Studies	Team Intern - NPO	Yes	Yes	Yes		B		Experience is relevant; however, time in relevant roles is limited.	Yes
C	Masters of Social Science	Program Advisor - Government	No	Yes	No		B		Has experience designing training material.	Yes
D	MBA	Project Coordinator - NPO	Yes	Yes	No		B		Limited project coordination experience related to corporate services.	Yes
E	Masters of Arts - Conflict Studies	Program Delivery Coordinator - NPO	No	Yes	No		B		Experience coordinating application processing and processing files.	Yes
F	Bachelor of Sciences	HR Manager - Private Sector	No	Maybe	Maybe		B		Developed and designed education materials. Grammar errors in cover letter.	Yes
G	Bachelor of Psychology	Research Writer - NPO	No	Yes	No			C	13 positions in 10 years. No related experience.	No

2. Selection Interviews

We all see the reports that say that employment interviews are not the most effective way to make hiring decisions. They are, however, by far still the number one selection method used by NPOs. Behavioral interviews are an effective tool for this. The Career Services department at Virginia Tech[v] offers the following:

Behavioral Interviewing

Behavioral interviewing is a technique used by employers to learn about your past behavior in particular situations. Why? Past behavior is a better predictor of

---

future behavior than is speculation (on your part) about how you would act in a hypothetical future situation.

Examples:

1. *Weak question: "Do you like working with people?" This question could be answered with a "yes" or "no" and is extremely vague. It begs the questions: What kinds of people (coworkers, clients)? Working how (teaching, serving, leading)? The answer is implied – most likely the interviewee is expected to say "yes." Thus, this question is poorly phrased and is likely to yield no useful information.*

2. *Better, but not best question: "If you had to work with an annoyed customer, what would you do?" Better because this specifies the type of person and the type of situation.*
    Not best because it calls on the interviewee to speculate; it's hypothetical. The candidate can likely come up with a predicted future behavior that is preferable, even if they did not behave that way in the past.

3. *Best format, which is not a question, but a statement calling for your response: "Tell me about a time that you had to deal with a disgruntled individual in a work situation."*
    Why this is best: The candidate must draw on past behavior, which is the best predictor of future behaviors.

3. Post-Interview Assessment

Upon completing the interview process you should conduct a post-interview assessment to determine the finalists and invite them for a second round of interviews, if required. Second round interviews may comprise:

- Situation simulation tests.
- Practical tests.
- Psychometrics tests.
- Intellectual aptitude tests.
- Performance tests.
- Interview with colleagues, peers, or additional management staff.

It is possible that some of this testing has been completed as part of the assessment stage.

4. Reference Checks

Talking to the candidate's former employers and co-workers will allow you to gain a better sense of their values, approach to work, and how they interact with others. Reference checks are a last opportunity to verify the accuracy of the information the candidate has provided, validate their personal suitability, and explore any areas of concern.

Prior to conducting reference checks you should inform the candidate you will be checking references. Some organizations ask that candidates provide written permission before contacting references. Be sure to find out if there is anyone the candidate would prefer you not speak to or if there are sensitivities required in checking certain references.

Here is a sample of questions for a reference check:

NPO – Sample Reference Form for a Project Officer

Candidate Name: *Person A*
Date:
Referee Information: *Name, Title, Organization, Contact Information*

1. *When did you work with Person A? How long was she employed with your organization? What was the reporting relationship?*

2. *What was Person A's role in your organizations? What were some of her duties under that title?*

3. *Would you rate her relative performance as above average, average, or below average and Why?*

4. *Can you please comment on the following skills:*

   - *Organization / Time Management skills*
   - *Professionalism*
   - *Written Communication Skills*
   - *Verbal Communication Skills*
   - *Punctuality/ Reliability*
   - *Degree of Supervision Required*
   - *Interpersonal skills?*

---

5. *How would you rate Person A's Project Management skills on a scale from 1-10 and Why?*

6. *Did Person A have any experience with related Project Management tools?*

7. *Can you think of an example of a great achievement she accomplished in her role? What impressed you the most about Person A?*

8. *What are Person A's greatest strengths?*

9. *What personal development opportunities would you recommend for Person A? Why?*

10. *Would you hire Person A or work with her again in a project management / coordination type of role?*

11. *Comments/Overall Impression*

5. Hiring Decision

Upon making your final decision evaluate the finalists against one another after rating them against the criteria in order to identify the best candidate based on skills, work characteristics and organizational fit.

The hiring decision should rely on five key dimensions:

1. Technical competencies, such as education, training, know-how, and experience.
2. Behavioral competencies, such as adaptability,

communications, creativity, and innovation.

3. Personal characteristics, such as interpersonal skills.
4. Motivation, including attitude and reactions during the interview.
5. References.

Rank the finalists on each of the five dimensions and make a final decision. Make a verbal offer of the position to the selected candidate. Send out rejection letters to all other candidates that were invited to the second round of interviews.

Hiring Tips – Realistic Previews[vi]

- Give potential job candidates a realistic, balanced job preview during the interviewing process.
- Hire candidates who understand the difficulties and challenges of your particular organization.

The Executive Director of a large homeless shelter we know likes to leave applicants for interview appointments sitting in their front lobby for a few extra minutes, mingling with the clientele of the Shelter. While it may sound cruel, she views it as a useful orientation to their unique work environment. Apparently, about a third of applicants choose to leave before the interview.

- Realistic job previews during the interview process greatly reduce misunderstandings staff may have about what the job actually entails.
- Realistic job previews are any method to give recruits a balanced picture of the job. Realistic job previews are typically brochures, videos, or per-

sonal presentations that inform recruits about both the positive and negative aspects of the job. Recruits form an accurate and realistic picture of the job.

- Many firms are in such a desperate need for staff that they only stress the positive aspects of the position.
- Applicants need to understand both the negative and positive aspects of the position in order to make an informed decision about whether the job is really something they want to pursue.

Corporate Culture in the Hiring Process

Culture is the environment that surrounds you at work all of the time. We also address corporate culture in Chapter 3 – Organization Design. It is a powerful element that shapes your work enjoyment, your work relationships, and your work processes. However, culture is something that you cannot actually see, except through its physical manifestations in your workplace. It is made up of the values, beliefs, underlying assumptions, attitudes, and behaviors shared by a group of people. Culture is the behavior that results when a group arrives at a set of rules for working together, rules generally unspoken and unwritten.

An organization's culture is made up of all of the life experiences each employee brings to the organization. Culture is especially influenced by the organization's founder, executives, and other managerial staff because of their role in decision-making and strategic direction.

92

Your bulletin board content, the company newsletter, the interaction of employees in meetings, and the way in which people collaborate speak volumes about your organizational culture.

People in every workplace talk about organizational culture, that mysterious word characterizing a work environment. One of the key questions and assessments, when employers interview a prospective employee, explores whether the candidate is a good cultural fit. Culture is difficult to define, but you generally know by gut feel when you have found an employee who appears to fit your culture.

Competing for the most qualified candidates can be intense, and persuading them to join your organization may be difficult. The final stages of the recruitment process involve selling your organization to potential employees to try and sway them to join your team.

Common Mistakes

Mistakes that recruiters often make when trying to market their NPO include:

- Using high-pressure tactics to try and persuade candidates to accept a job offer. For example, offering a job on the spot and asking for a response within a day can often backfire on the organization and deter a candidate from accepting the offer.
- Overselling the organization and creating false expectations can have a negative effect. Employers should be honest about any factors that could

present future obstacles to job candidates.

▪ Waiting too long to extend an initial job offer.
  • Candidates are often applying for multiple positions. Waiting to extend your offer to your ideal candidate means they could easily be hired on by another organization in the interim.

This is one of our pet peeves in NPO staffing. Sometimes the Hiring Manager will not have a sense of urgency in the hiring or appreciate that it is a time sensitive process. While they may not be in a hurry, waiting to interview or to extend a job offer sometimes means that they lose top talent to other employers – even in times of economic uncertainly. It means that other candidates must be interviewed or even starting the entire recruiting process over again.

Nonprofits should be on the hunt for talent all of the time. This business requirement may mean it is time for you to rebuild your recruitment strategy. Often organizations are only scanning the labor market and available talent pool when they have a position that they need to fill. In order to secure talent within your organization, you must be scanning the talent pool at all times.

Recruiting Sources for NPOs

Two great sources of people for NPOs are the Job Posting Boards at Charity Village in Canada and Idealist. org in the United States.

Notes

[i] "The Employe Value Proposition: 6 Things You Need to Know." (Recruiters Network, 2003).

[ii] Brett Minchington, *Employer Brand Leadership – A Global Perspective* (Collective Learning Australia, 2010).

[iii] Human Resource Advice, BCJobs.ca (2011).

[iv] Ibid.

[v] Career Services, Virginia Tech (2011).

[vi] "The War for Talent," (CAmagazine.com, 2007).

5

Compensation

Show Me the Money

Are you paying your employees properly? Payroll costs usually represent 60 to 85% of the total operating budget for most NPOs. Spending your money carefully is, therefore, vitally important.

Compensation can be viewed as a tool, a tool to effectively reward employees in order to achieve maximum productivity. You need to decide if it is a blunt instrument or a precision tool.

The objectives of this chapter are to:

▪ Understand the components of compensation in the context of total rewards.
▪ Learn the various elements involved in properly paying your employees.
▪ Learn how to create a pay structure.
▪ Familiarize the reader with the essential components of the Base Pay Model, including job descriptions, job evaluation, the four types of equity, internal salary structure, external market position, and salary administration.
▪ Explain the process involved in integrating these components and building a core compensation program.

This chapter is divided into several sections:

A. Compensation 101: The Basics.
B. Non-Profit Salary Dilemmas. (*Yes, there is more than one.*)
C. Compensation Planning.
D. Notes on Executive Compensation Reviews.
E. Sample Compensation Policy Statement.

A. <u>Compensation 101: The Basics</u>

What is compensation? It can be defined two ways: as payment or reward for performance of a service, or as the reward that employees receive in exchange for their work. Compensation includes all forms of financial returns, tangible services and benefits employees receive as part of an employment relationship.

The Objectives of Compensation

According to WorldatWork (The Total Rewards Organization), the objectives of compensation include:

- Internal equity.
- External competitiveness (employer's viewpoint).
- External equity (employee's viewpoint).
- Performance incentives.
- Ability to pay (employer's viewpoint).
- Compliance with laws and regulations.
- Administrative efficiency.[i]

The Pay Model

The elements of a Total Compensation Program are outlined in the following figure:

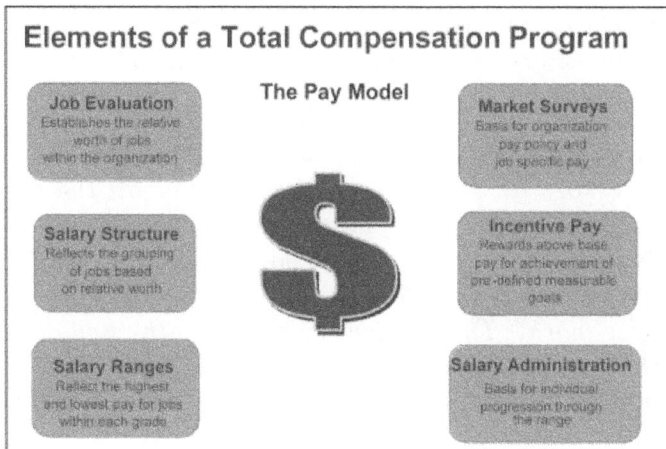

Elements of a Total Compensation Program

The Pay Model

Job Evaluation
Establishes the relative worth of jobs within the organization

Market Surveys
Basis for organization pay policy and job specific pay

Salary Structure
Reflects the grouping of jobs based on relative worth

Incentive Pay
Rewards above base pay for achievement of pre-defined measurable goals

Salary Ranges
Reflect the highest and lowest pay for jobs within each grade

Salary Administration
Basis for individual progression through the range

Fairness

A key issue in compensation is what we call the Fairness Dilemma.

Your compensation program must be fair. But what is fair? Is equal (identical) treatment to all fair? Or, is unequal treatment more fair? Employees expect fairness. But does your Employee Manual actually use the word "fair"? Do your employment contracts?

In our classes and presentations on Compensation we use an interesting exercise to drive home the importance of fairness, and employees' intrinsic expectation that the employer should / will treat them in a fair manner. We take one side of the room and ask for a volunteer (which is an exercise unto itself). We ask the volunteer to pretend that this is a university classroom setting and that there is a chalkboard at the front.

I explain that the university has recently required that all professors (in this case, me) have to clean the chalkboard at the end of every class. I do not wish to get my hands dirty, so I'm hiring the volunteer to do this task for me. The pay is $20 cash, paid in advance, for five minutes work. The university supplies the brushes. I ask the volunteer (now my employee) if they agree that this is a good deal. After a discussion, they always do.

I then go to the other side of the room and explain that (in this pretend world) I'm now using the chalkboard on their side of the room and I need a second volunteer to be my employee to clean this chalkboard. The employment

arrangements will be the same as those for the first per-
son. Except, I am going to pay the second volunteer $50
for the task, paid in advance, for five minutes work. The
volunteer happily agrees.

At this point, there are gasps and a moan coming from
the other side of the room and the first employee is glar-
ing at me. I wander over and innocently ask if anything
is wrong. The first volunteer is invariably quite upset
because the second one is earning 150% more for the
same job. I respond by saying, "Hey, we had an arrange-
ment. You were quite happy three minutes ago; nothing
in my contract with you has changed. What's the prob-
lem?" The problem, of course, is that they have made an
internal / external equity comparison, seen that someone
else is getting paid more (far more) for the same job and
they are not happy.

This happens every day in the real world – employees
make internal and external comparisons. However,
how many organizations put in their hiring letters or
employment contracts a commitment to pay what the
market is paying? It may or may not be in your Compensation Policy or HR Manual, but it is never in an
employment contract. Even though it's not written
down, your employees fully expect you to be fair.

The same principle has been expressed far more formally by academics:

"The more an employee will perceive a high level of
internal equity (in comparison with other employees of
the same department and/or the same company) and

external equity (in comparison with individuals occupying a similar job in other organizations) in regard to issues such as compensation and benefits, performance evaluation, and promotions, the less s/he will intend to leave his/her current employer. It seems clear that the notion of equity, both internal and external, must be considered as a critical component of a corporate retention strategy.[xii]

Types of Equity

In the following figure, there are four types of equity in compensation. In our terms, equity means fairness.

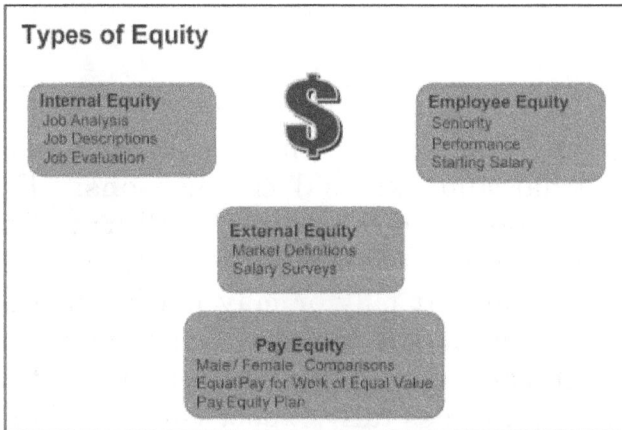

Types of Equity

Internal Equity
Job Analysis
Job Descriptions
Job Evaluation

$

Employee Equity
Seniority
Performance
Starting Salary

External Equity
Market Definitions
Salary Surveys

Pay Equity
Male/Female Comparisons
Equal Pay for Work of Equal Value
Pay Equity Plan

Internal Equity is the term used to describe fair compensation with respect to how different positions within the organization relate to each other. It is the relative ranking of all jobs to each other based on their value to the organization. Internal job-to-job comparison is based on job analysis, job descriptions and job evaluation / classification.

External Equity is the term used to describe fair and competitive compensation with respect to the market value of a job. It is the average level at which your organization pays relative to the outside labor market. This is determined through market definitions (defining your relevant labor market), salary surveys, and your pay policy decision (where you wish to pay relative to the market).

Employee Equity refers to fairness in compensation among employees in the same job, or whose positions are classified in the same job grade or level. Again, fairness does not mean identical pay. Appropriate differences in employee levels within the same salary range can be based on seniority, performance and different starting salaries.

Pay Equity is the difference in pay between males and females. At first, Pay Equity meant equal pay for equal work (the premise that individuals should be paid the same wage for the same kind of work regardless of gender, age, color or religion). The concept later evolved to equal pay for work of equal value. Women and men must receive equal pay when they are doing substantially the same kind of work, requiring the same skill, effort and responsibility performed under similar working conditions in the same establishment. In many jurisdictions a formal Pay Equity Plan is legally required. This plan may be a direct requirement for many NPOs.

B. <u>Non-Profit Salary Dilemmas (Part 1)</u>

NPOs face a dilemma when it comes to salaries – they are not government and they are not the private sector. They are in the middle. So what does their Compensation program look like? Do they pay like government – that is, provide annual step increases based primarily on tenure and experience? Or, do they pay like the private sector, with a strong emphasis on performance and merit pay?

This is a pervasive issue. We are constantly asked about it. Every single CEO, Executive Director, and Director of Finance and Administration we meet with about Compensation raises this question.

Many NPOs desire the productivity that pay-for-performance programs can generate; but they often lack the discipline and willpower necessary to enforce such policies.

Pay for Performance (or Not) in NPOs

A policy on pay for performance typically refers to the relative emphasis that an NPO wishes to place on rewarding individual employee performance. For example, should one staff member be paid differently from another if one has better performance? How much differently? Should more productive teams of employees receive higher annual increases than less productive teams? These are more than just philosophical questions that management must answer.

The following section outlines the relative advantages and disadvantages of two different approaches to compensation philosophy: pay-for-performance (also called merit pay) versus straight across-the-board economic increases (also called COLA – Cost of Living Adjustment). It assesses which type of program (or combination) might be most appropriate for a given NPO.

Summary of Relative Differences

The following table provides a short point-form summary of the relative differences between two distinct approaches to annual salary increases: pay-for-performance versus straight economic increases (COLA). These approaches can be viewed as being at opposite ends of a spectrum.

Element	Pay-for-performance	COLA
Background Data Required	Annual employee performance appraisals, plus the CPI data noted on the right	Annual Consumer Price Index (CPI) movement for local market, plus data on average wage increases in local market
Ease of Operation	Complex	Straightforward
Degree of Equity	Adjustments vary by employee	Percentage adjustments are the same for everybody
	Rewards higher performers; does not reward low performers	Higher performers rewarded the same as low performers

Element	Pay-for-performance	COLA
Erosion of Employee Salary Due to Inflation	Higher performers receive an adjustment greater than inflation. Poor performers lag behind inflation. Average performers stay even.	All employees stay even with inflation by getting an annual COLA

Actual Practice

Many NPOs blend these two approaches. They reward employees on the basis of performance (following an annual performance appraisal) by providing annual merit increases which effectively have a cost-of-living adjustment built in. Higher level performers receive slightly larger increases (as much as 1 or 2 percent more) than poorer performers.

The question is: Will the monetary motivation of 1 to 2 percent be sufficient? Does the organization wish to formally link rewards (annual pay increases) to the achievement of individual and organizational goals to a greater extent than the current practice?

The degree of emphasis to be placed on performance is an important policy decision, since it directly affects employees' attitudes and work behaviors. Recognition of their contributions also affects employees' perception of management's fairness. They need to understand the basis for judging performance in order to believe that their pay is fair.

Pay-for-Performance

Pay-for-performance (also called merit pay) links rewards to the achievement of organization objectives. It provides an opportunity for employees to receive re-earnable financial rewards (larger annual increases) based on the achievement of predefined, measurable performance goals related to the organization's success.

A key guiding principle of a pay-for-performance program is alignment. There needs to be considerable alignment between the following elements:

1. The defined (and communicated) corporate goals of the organization.
2. The measurement of how these goals are accomplished (and communication of same).
3. Determination of the employee behaviors that are needed to support and drive these goals.
4. The identification and measurement of these behaviors through performance appraisals (objective setting and assessment).
5. The calibration of economic rewards (annual salary adjustments) to the performance appraisal results.

Other factors are also needed. Demonstrable CEO and organizational commitment to the alignment of these five elements is vital. The creation and nurturing of a corporate culture of goal setting, business planning, program measurement, and individual personal accountability is a hallmark of an effective pay-for-performance system; as is a commitment to rewarding top performers, even when overall program objectives are not met, or when economic conditions are not supportive.

The advantages of a well run pay-for-performance system are as follows. It:

- Clarifies performance expectations.
- Improves individual performance.
- Rewards employees for achieving performance results and exhibiting behaviors that are aligned with the mission and goals.
- Improves employee satisfaction with work and pay.
- Rewards performance rather than seniority or skills.
- Provides rewards commensurate with contributions (such as bigger pay increases for stronger performers, and very low increases for poor performers).
- Assists in attracting and retaining highly motivated employees.

The disadvantages are:

- The effort required to manage the guidelines and factors outlined above.
- The work involved in upgrading the organization's performance appraisal process.
- Training supervisors and managers on the documentation and assessment of performance standards.
- Communicating the plan.
- Managing the process on an annual basis.
- The process may be focused on the individual and does not necessarily reward team performance.

Annual Economic Increases / Cost of Living Adjustments

By comparison, cost of living adjustments give employees the same percentage salary increase across the board. This increase is given to everyone, regardless of their performance.

Employees often compare their pay increases to changes in their cost of living. They may argue that increasing living costs justify equivalent adjustments in their pay by the employer.

It is important to distinguish among three related concepts:

- Change in an employee's cost of living.
- Change in the products and service (consumer) markets.
- Change in wages/salaries in the labor market.

Changes in an employee's cost of living are a function of their personal expense budget. Price changes over time in the product and service markets are measured by the Consumer Price Index (CPI). Tying salary changes to the CPI is called indexing. Changes in the labor market are measured through annual salary surveys.

It is up to the organization to determine a combined local labor market policy line and annual cost of living adjustment determination in their industry and geographic location.

The primary advantage of COLA is that employees feel their salaries are holding ground against the steady erosion of buying power caused by inflation. The main disadvantage is that the organization has no means by which to distinguish the rewards given to low versus high performers.

The following points are worth highlighting:

- There are relative advantages to both of these approaches, merit pay and economic adjustments.
- Most NPOs occupy the middle ground. That is, as not-for-profit organizations, they are neither in the public sector nor the private. They are not government and are equally not driven by the profit motive.
- A pure pay-for-performance system is incongruous with most NPO cultures.
- A pure COLA environment may also not be in line with existing policies.

NPOs may wish to consider a pay-for-performance philosophy along the lines of the following example:

Salaries are a large component of our operating budget and represent the major source of income for most employees. It is important that salary determinations are made in a thoughtful, sensitive way.

ABC Non-Profit's pay administration program supports the following management objectives:

- *Attracting highly qualified employees*
- *Retaining productive, effective and satisfied employees*

- *Providing an environment in which employees are encouraged to grow and develop their job skills.*

We strive to pay employee salaries that represent three perspectives:

- *Internal equity – which ensures that differences in salary grades correctly reflect differences in the relative value of job responsibility.*
- *External equity – which ensures that salary ranges at ABC Non-Profit compare favorably to those of similar employers in the National Capital region from year to year.*
- *The fiscal realities of the agency.*

ABC Non-Profit is committed to rewarding employees on the basis of performance. The Agency will pay merit increases to meritorious employees each year. This presumes that individual differences in job performance are measurable and is based on the premise that superior performance will be encouraged and rewarded.

B. Non-Profit Salary Dilemmas (Part 2)

A completely different challenge for some NPOs is the limitations placed on salary levels by donors: government, foundation and private donors.

Either the donor will place a cap on the maximum salary payable to incumbents in a program they have funded, or they will specify the exact rate of pay. This inhibits the ability of the NPO's management to recruit and pay for employees within their overall Pay Policy framework.

It can also impact Internal Equity. We have a client organization that employs about 70 staff. They host and operate a variety of operational programs. Many of these programs are directly funded by external donors.

In several cases, the donor organizations mandate the level of pay of staff working in the program. Given that some programs are more generously funded than others, this leads to variances in salary scales and pay for similar positions (case workers, program coordinators, counselors) from one program to another. This creates a serious internal equity challenge for the organization.

C. <u>Compensation Planning</u>

Compensation Planning is:

- The framework for your NPO's Total Rewards Strategy (TRS).
- A strategic endeavor: developing a plan and aligning it with your mission, goals and business objectives.
- A process which must include consideration of your Compensation philosophy and your organization's ability to pay.

Why is it important? Paying your employees too much is a waste of money. Paying them too little is also a waste of money, since it can lead to turnover and increased recruiting, hiring and training costs. Paying new employees whatever they ask for is Wild West management, with a similar body count. You have to do it properly.

A well designed Compensation Plan is a tool. It will support and contribute to your organization's success, ensure employees view total rewards as valuable, and reduce the number of dissatisfied employees (at least with their pay) and the legal consequences of their dissatisfaction.

Compensation Planning starts with determining your core attitudes and approach to pay.

- It outlines the intent, objectives and priorities of the Compensation Plan.
- It's the organization's vision of Compensation. What do you want to accomplish?
- It provides the foundation for Compensation Plan design and administration.
- It asks:
  - How does our current compensation strategy support the goals of our NPO?
  - Where do we sit regarding compensation in our sector and market?
  - Do we demonstrate fair, equitable, and competitive pay practices?
  - How do each employee's talents link to the organization's goals?
- These questions should be answered in a way that considers every person in the organization, from the janitor to the CEO.[iii]

Communicating

The Compensation Communication Dilemma is a key aspect of Compensation Planning. This decision is unique to every organization. How much do you tell your staff?

Should staff know:

- Their own salary? (*Presumably.*)
- Other employee salaries?
- Their job grade?
- Their salary range?
- How they progress through the range?
- When and how annual salary increases are managed?
- Your Compensation Philosophy / Policy?
- Your Pay Policy Position?

Communicating Your Plan

You need to <u>sell</u> your Compensation Plan to employees. The best designed plan won't be effective if the people who are supposed to benefit from it don't really understand how it works. No other topic is more important to an employee in his/her relationship with the organization.

Effective communication of your Compensation Plan can boost employees' satisfaction with their pay, enhance the commitment level of employees to the organization, and improve trust in management.

Poor communication can lead to misinformation seeping into the organization and employees internalizing incorrect information, whether it's valid or not. It can also damage employee morale and create a misalignment of employee and company objectives.

Top Five Mistakes in Compensation Planning by NPOs

> *In our consulting experience, we have found:*
>
> 1) *Many organizations don't do compensation planning at all.*
> 2) *The plan does not align with the organization's strategy, goals, objectives, and culture.*
> 3) *Management does not effectively communicate the plan to employees.*
> 4) *The plan does not remain consistent or constant.*
> 5) *Management uses inappropriate methods in determining individual pay.*

D. Executive Compensation Reviews

While our firm may be hired by the senior management of our clients, we are often called on to present our findings and rationale to the Boards of Directors of these organizations as they exercise their fiduciary responsibility. This is particularly true in the case of Executive Compensation.

Elements of Executive Compensation

- There are five basic elements in Executive Compensation: base salary, employee benefits, perquisites, short-term incentives, and long-term incentives.
- Long-term incentives are usually not offered in the Not-for-Profit sector. Our focus in this sector is normally just on base salary.

- In Executive Compensation reviews in this sector, we usually survey for actual base salaries. Most senior executive positions do not have a salary range per se.

Job Matching

The key to any survey is job matching. It is the most common method of ensuring comparability of data. Job matching looks for comparable positions with similar job content and responsibility. The key factors are industry sector and geographic location. These comprise the comparative labor market – which in this case is the NPO sector.

Within this sector we look for comparable scope. This scope can be assessed by size of operating budget and number of employees. Statistically speaking, sector, revenue, budget and staff size are normally the major correlating factors driving executive base pay.

Interestingly, however, there is sometimes minimal correlation between revenue / staff size and base pay in this sector. Some small organizations pay relatively highly, while some larger organizations pay far less. A wide variance in base pay levels may appear to be the reality of this particular market.

On the other hand, a 2011 salary survey in the United States by Guidestar, reported in The Chronicle of Philanthropy, reported a standard progression in median pay for NPO chief executives.[iv]

Median Pay for Chief Executives	
Budget of Organization	**Overall Median**
More than $50-million	$422,381
$25-million to $49.9-million	$247,309
$10-million to $24.9-million	$184,545
$5-million to $9.9-million	$147,712
$2.5-million to $4.9-million	$117,724
$1-million to $2.49-million	$90,909
$500,000 to $999,999	$67,291
$250,000 to $499,999	$53,000
Less than $250,000	$41,800

Pay Policy

Another aspect of Executive Compensation is the organization's Pay Policy Position – that is, Where do you position your salaries relative to those paid by your comparative labor market?

Most NPOs will aim to pay overall at the average (or mean) of the survey data. A related data point is the 50th percentile of the data, or P50 for short. This data point is usually close to the average (although statistically a separate measure). So, the phrase "being competitive" means P50 in HR terminology.

Some organizations will pay less than the market average or P50 because they either don't know what the market is paying or because of budgetary considerations. Other organizations, however, deliberately choose to pay more than the market average, recognizing that average means half of the data is higher. This is often because they need or want to attract better than average candidates or candidates with unique or high demand skill sets.

In some cases, an organization will deliberately choose to pay more than the market average in order to recognize the value of and to retain a high performing employee – especially at the executive level. In these cases they may pay at the 60th or 75th percentile of the market data for that position.

E. Sample Compensation Policy Statement

It is our goal at the ABC Non-Profit to compensate staff in a manner that is fair, reflective of the external market, and provides recognition for the achievement of individual goals, corporate objectives, and professional competency. Specifically, our goal is to achieve the following objectives:

- *Internal equity based on fairness and consistency*
- *External equity and competitiveness*
- *Increased performance and productivity*
- *Compliance with laws and regulations*
- *Administrative efficiency*

The following policy summarizes the ABC Non-Profit Compensation Program. The program consists of two components:

- *Pay Structure*
- *Salary Increases*

The ABC Non-Profit reserves the right to modify and adjust the policy as required to meet economic and business conditions.

A. Pay Structure

The pay structure is the foundation of our employee Compensation Program. It is based on a hierarchy of jobs, job grades, and a salary range assigned to each job grade.

Each job at the ABC Non-Profit has a current and up-to-date job description. Each job has been assessed and assigned to a job grade. The grade was based on an assessment of job content (skill, effort, responsibility and working conditions) and the premise that the greater the worth of a job, the higher its job grade.

The ABC Non-Profit Pay Structure consists of eight job grades, each with a salary range containing a minimum, midpoint, and maximum.

- *The minimum is usually the lowest rate of pay for positions in each job grade.*
- *The midpoint is based on the Market Line (the average rates of pay for equivalent positions in the local labor market). It is midway between the minimum and maximum. It is the job rate, the pay rate at which (ideally) a qualified employee with good performance can expect to achieve over time.*
- *The maximum is the highest rate of pay for positions in each job grade.*

It is the policy of the ABC Non-Profit to pay competitively with the external labor market. The salary range values are, therefore, designed to be equitable with the external labor market.

Periodically, market salary data will be reviewed by the ABC Non-Profit to ensure that pay rates remain competitive. Based on the results of this information, adjustments may be made to the salary ranges in the pay structure from time to time. Pay structure adjustments will raise the minimums, midpoints, and maximums of the salary ranges to bring them in line with current market levels.

The salary ranges may also be periodically adjusted to reflect changes in the cost of living.

B. Application of the Pay Structure

Placement for new hires:
- *New hires are placed within the range at a salary that is reflective of their previous experience in similar roles. This placement will normally be between the salary range minimum and midpoint.*

Promotion to a job in a higher level:
- *If an employee receives a promotion to a job in a higher level, the incumbent will be placed at the minimum of the higher salary range or will be provided an increase of 5%, whichever is greater. This placement is an industry best practice.*

Job re-classification:
- *If the duties of a job change and the position is re-classified upward, the ABC Non-Profit will ensure that the incumbent is placed in the new salary range at the minimum of the higher range or will be provided an increase of 5%, whichever is greater.*

- *If the duties of a job change and the position is re-classified downward, the ABC Non-Profit will ensure that the incumbent is red-circled at their current rate of pay until such time that the range is adjusted (due to cost of living) to the point where the incumbent's rate of pay falls within the salary range.*

C. Salary Increases

On an annual basis the Executive Director, in consultation with the Compensation Committee of the Board of Directors, will determine the overall annual budget for salaries.

There are a number of factors that contribute to the Executive Director's decision – the consumer price index, the anticipated adjustments of similar organizations, the overall performance of the organization, individual employee performance, and changes (either financial or non-financial) to the Employee Benefits package.

Our Compensation Policy for annual salary increases is based on Merit or Pay for Performance. The ABC Non-Profit believes in rewarding employees for job performance. Employees are eligible for a salary increase if they achieve their stated performance objectives and demonstrate professional competency in their job.

Pay-for-performance (also called merit pay) links rewards to the achievement of the organization's objectives. It provides an opportunity for employees to receive re-earnable financial rewards (larger annual increases) based on the achievement of predefined, measurable performance goals related to our success.

All employees who have completed their annual perfor-mance review and who have been with the ABC Non-Profit for a full calendar year are eligible for a salary increase. Annual salary increases are dependent on the completion of the Performance Review process in February and will be awarded each year in April.

D. Progress through the Range

Progress through the range is defined as base pay movement over time for individual performance, competency develop-ment, skill acquisition, and/or job growth. Employees will progress through their respective salary ranges based on meeting performance expectations, as determined through the annual performance review process. If employees do not demonstrate an increase in individual competencies, then progression pay adjustments will be withheld. The progression through the range adjustment may not exceed the maximum of the salary range.

E. Merit Pay Matrix

A Merit Pay Matrix is used by the ABC Non-Profit to link salary increases to annual job performance and employees' current position within the salary range. The following fig-ures will be adjusted from year to year. They include and reflect both an annual cost-of-living allowance and pay for performance.

Performance Level	*Position in the Salary Range*		
	Minimum to Midpoint	*Midpoint*	*Midpoint to Maximum*
Outstanding	*6%*	*5%*	*4%*
Consistently Exceeds Standards	*5%*	*4%*	*3%*
Consistently Meets Standards	*4%*	*3%*	*2%*
Occasionally Meets Standards	*0% - 3%*	*No Increase*	*No Increase*
Does Not Meet Standards	*No Increase*	*No Increase*	*No Increase*

The Merit Pay Matrix has the following objectives:

- *To accelerate high performers through their respective salary ranges, particularly those who are in the lower end of the salary range.*
- *To allow satisfactory performers to progress into the middle of the salary range.*
- *To hold lower performers in the lower part of their respective salary range until such time as their performance improves.*

F. Awarding Annual Salary Increases

The process for awarding annual salary increases is as follows:

1. *In November of each year, the ABC Non-Profit will determine the increase amounts (or percentages) for*

> *annual salary increases to staff. The percentage figures in the Merit Pay Matrix example above will be reviewed annually.*
>
> 2. *The annual salary increase amounts (or percentage) will be linked to the performance management ratings and will clearly identify the level of required performance for each increase in salary.*
>
> 3. *Upon the completion of each employee's Performance Plan and Review, a calibration meeting will be held among the Senior Management Team in order to assign an increase amount (or percentage) for individual employees. Directors' increases will be determined by the Executive Director.*
>
> 4. *Upon approval, the Executive Director will prepare salary increase letters for each employee placing a copy of the letter in each employee file.*
>
> 5. *The Executive Director will communicate the salary increase amount to the employee. (These tasks may be delegated to the Director, Human Resources.)*

Notes

[i] WorldatWork

[ii] Paré and Tremblay, "École des Hautes Études Commerciales" (August, 2000).

[iii] Stacey Carroll, PayScale.com

[iv] Guidestar and Chronicle of Philanthropy (Washington, D.C., September 2011).

6

Employee Retention

Will the People You Hire Stay?

As employers, NPOs have several choices in terms of employment options: full time, part time, permanent, temporary, casual, or contract (see Chapter 4 – Staffing).

Employees, on the other hand, have at least nine ways to leave their job. These are:

1. Walk away (job abandonment).
2. Death.
3. Be demoted (constructive dismissal).
4. Be fired.
5. Be laid off (permanently).

6.   Retire.
7.   Transfer.
8.   Promotion.
9.   Resign.

While most of these actions are at the employer's discretion, it is number 9 that strikes fear into the heart of managers and HR professionals.

Susan, the Manager of Member Programs, walks into your office at 4:00 p.m. appearing a little nervous. She advises that she is resigning. She has found a job with another NPO. You haven't seen this coming and you are shocked. She is your best performer. Worse, your annual conference is in six weeks and Susan is the lead organizer. What happened?

Your NPO's ability to achieve its business mandate and serve its members is highly dependent on the performance of your employees. Unanticipated changes in your employee resource pool can have devastating business impacts – disrupted projects, overruns on schedules and budgets, quality issues, and loss of corporate memory, to name just a few.

While some turnover is generally considered a good thing, what concerns managers the most is the unwanted and unexpected separation of high-performing talent.

Do You Have a Retention Deficit?

How many of your top performers are simply biding their time – waiting until the market improves before bolting to the next job?

There is a term called "warm chair attrition" which describes this phenomenon. Employees suffering from warm chair attrition have already left their jobs, at least mentally. Their physical departure only awaits the first uptick in the job market. Look down the hall, how many of your people currently fit into this category?

When staff do leave, it's generally not the laggards who go. The first people out the door will be the folks with the most options – undoubtedly, the best employees in your organization.

Why is it Always the Good People Who Leave?

Data gathered from exit interviews highlights the following reasons why people leave their employer:

- Job Dissatisfaction
  This is the number one reason why good people leave. It is a catchall term, but if people are unhappy, feel undervalued or unappreciated, they will soon leave.

- Lack of Challenge
  Good people need to have their skills used and tested constantly. If challenge is missing, they will soon be missing as well.

- Lack of Confidence in the Organization
  This reason often goes hand-in-hand with lack of challenge. If the corporate culture or the organization's image is not deserving of respect, good employees will soon find another, better environment.

- Dissatisfaction with Co-Workers
  Personality differences within the staff can cause people to leave. It is important to consider the chemistry of people who must work together as a team. Mixing aggressive and passive people, for example, can lead to disruptive personality clashes. This can be mitigated with proper training and coaching.

- Compensation
  Many studies have shown that compensation is usually way down on the list of reasons why good people leave. If the only right thing in a person's job is the pay received, no amount of money will keep that employee.[i]

Top 10 Clues Your Best Employees are Leaving

1. *They start dressing better.*
2. *They take lunches at different times.*
3. *Their production drops off.*
4. *They seem "quiet" or "down".*
5. *They request vacation one day at a time.*
6. *They are "sick" more often.*
7. *They stop championing their positions.*
8. *They stop volunteering.*

> 9.   *They get more incoming phone calls than usual, and number 10.*
> 10. *They ask you for a reference.*[ii]

Retention Getters

So how do you get people to stay? The ability to retain staff so that they can provide effective contributions to your NPO's success is an outcome of your HR practices. But what works, and what doesn't work?

More money is not the answer. In any case, today's NPOs are unlikely to have more money. Non-monetary HR practices that an NPO can employ to increase commitment and decrease turnover include:

- Non-monetary recognition of performance (try saying thank you).
- Empowerment (increased responsibility for work and decision making).
- Fairness (equitable rules and procedures).
- Employee development (job rotation, mentoring, training).
- Work-life policies (flextime, flexible leave practices).
- Information sharing (communicate, communicate, communicate).

For most professionals, a significant portion of their motivation is derived from the recognition they receive from their managers for a job well done and the feeling that they are truly an important part of the organization.

Training is too often seen as a perk when it should be viewed as an essential investment in the intellectual capital of the organization. Training, coaching, developmental assignments and job rotation programs send a clear message that management is seeking to establish a long-term relationship with employees. Managers must help employees shape and direct their careers, so they can gain experience within the NPO rather than outside it. Your NPO's ability to do this, however, is a function of its size.

An important retention factor is quality of the boss – how staff are managed. Employees will often leave a job because of a poor supervisor.

So how do you rate as a boss?

A recent survey found that the top retention techniques (by degree of effectiveness) are:

1. Challenging work assignments.
2. Favorable work environment.
3. Flextime.
4. Additional vacation time.
5. Support for career / family values.
6. High-quality supervision and leadership.
7. Visionary leadership.
8. Cross-functional assignments, tuition and training reimbursement.[iii]

Treat your staff with R.E.S.P.E.C.T. In the HR context, this acronym stands for:

- **R**elate to your employees.
- **E**ngage and communicate.
- **S**upport personal needs.
- **P**ersonalize their development.
- **E**ncourage them.
- **C**ompensate fairly.
- **T**rust them.[iv]

Our Experience

The suggestions above all sound like "no brainers" and are intuitively obvious. However, we have seen NPOs where:

- *Very little news about the organization, its goals and its track record is ever communicated to employees.*
- *The Executive Director overvalues face time, and patrols the office at 4:30 p.m. making note of the stalwarts still hard at work.*
- *Favoritism by executives results in the termination of targeted (out of favor) employees on a regular basis.*
- *The Executive Director will walk into a meeting room and say hello to the visitors (us consultants) and ignore the staff sitting beside us. We have seen the same in elevators.*
- *Policies are inconsistently applied among departments; for example, on an afternoon with a raging blizzard outside, staff in one department are allowed to go home early while staff in another department (not one operationally critical) are forced to stay until 5:00 p.m.*
- *Policies are inconsistently applied by supervisors; for example, an employee is allowed to take a Friday off because she is in a wedding party the next day. Two weeks later, a co-worker is denied the exact same request.*

- *The office is still crowded with staff at 5:00 p.m. on a Friday in July. The staff are afraid to leave until the Directors go home first.*
- *With a January budget deadline looming, executives delay and dither over financial planning decisions from September to December, and then force staff to cancel Christmas vacations to rush the budget through.*

These actions drive employees crazy! And prompt them to dust off their resume.

More Retention Getters

What else can you do? Consider the following HR programs:

A. Performance Measurement

This should include persistent and accurate feedback (both formal and informal), the annual traditional performance appraisal, and 360-degree performance assessments (where appropriate).

B. Compensation and Benefits Systems

These systems are addressed in detail in Chapter 5 – Compensation. Options include bonuses, variable compensation, market-anchored compensation (to be competitive with other NPOs in your sector and geographic location), flexible benefits, and sabbaticals (these can be self-funded).

C. Learning and Development

Frank and frequent communication between an employee and manager or mentor about career development activities is vital. The amount of development offered is a critical consideration in an employee's decision to stay or leave. Activities include:

- Identifying learning and development needs.
- Development plans.
- Line of sight career growth.
- Learning to enhance current skills or to develop additional skills.
- Competency training.
- Tuition reimbursement.
- Training programs.
- Use of mentors.

D. Recognition Programs

These are programs that allow managers to recognize and reward outstanding or exemplary performance, such as: non-monetary rewards (including birthday cards and event tickets), awards, monetary rewards including performance bonuses, and basic recognition activities (like saying thank you, sending a reinforcing memo, or sharing a $100 voucher to take a spouse out for dinner).

E. Sense of Community

Leaders who are successful in retaining their staff recognize the key role played by a sense of belonging and community within the organization:

- Management communications.
- MBWA (Management by walking around).
- Keeping messages consistent.
- Lunch with the Executive Director for all new employees.
- Executive chats, group breakfasts.
- Social activities.
- Town hall meetings.

We have noticed over the years that executives fall into two camps – those that know their staff well and those that don't.

When we arrive at an NPO's office for a meeting we are usually offered coffee. We often accompany the executive to get the coffee, down the hall, around a few corners to the lunch room. During that trip and in the lunch room, the executives (with consultants in tow) will encounter other employees.

Some executives will completely ignore the staff, focused on the task at hand. With other executives, however, the coffee trip takes over ten minutes. They cheerily greet each and every employee they see, and inquire about their weekend plans and how the spouse and kids (knowing all their names) are doing.

While this may be a function of personality, clearly the second set of executives' employees feel far more connected to the organization.

F. Lifestyle Accommodation

Accommodation can include a casual dress code (within reason) and casual Fridays.

At Friday meetings with NPOs, we are often the only people not wearing jeans.

Work scheduling options that we like include accommodating work / time arrangements such as flexible start and end times, compressed work weeks (such as a four-day week), and bi-weekly schedules of nine days, with every second Friday off. All of these, of course, have to meet operational requirements for program delivery and client accessibility.

We are also big fans of summer hours.

Notes

---

[i] E.C. Pressler, Jr., "Why Good People Leave Jobs" (BankersOnline.com,1991).
[ii] F. John Reh, "Are Your Top People Ready to Leave You?" (Management.About.com, 2004).
[iii] Patrick Thibodeau, "Survey: Above All Else, IT Workers Need Challenge," (Survey of Hiring and Retention Practices by the American Electronics Association, Computerworld, January 2001).
[iv] "Managing for the Retention of IT Professionals" (Management Workshop, Interpersonal Technology Group, Inc., Rockville Centre, New York, 2003).

7

Succession Planning

Who's Next?

Succession planning is the flexible, long term, developmental view of management staffing for NPOs. It is a part of HR Planning. A key aspect of overall HR Planning is having a systematic process for defining future management requirements, identifying candidates and matching this demand to supply as a basis for future planning.

What do the following people have in common?

- *Donald Terner, President, Bridge Housing Corp., San Francisco, CA.*
- *Robert E. Donovan, President and Chief Executive*

> *Officer, Abb Inc., Norwalk, CT.*
> - *Claudio Elia, Chairman and Chief Executive Officer, Air & Water Technologies Corp., Somerville, NJ.*
> - *Stuart Tholan, President, Bechtel-Europe/Africa/Middle East/Southwest Asia, San Francisco, CA.*
> - *John A. Scoville, Chairman, Harza Engineering Co., Chicago, IL.*
> - *Leonard Pieroni, Chairman and Chief Executive Officer, Parsons Corp., Pasadena, CA.*
> - *Barry L. Conrad, Chairman and Chief Executive Officer, Barrington Group, Miami, FL.*
> - *Paul Cushman III, Chairman and Chief Executive Officer, Riggs International Banking Corp., Washington, D.C.*
> - *Robert A. Whittaker, Chairman and Chief Executive Officer, Foster Wheeler Energy International, Clifton, NJ.*
> - *Frank Maier, President, Ensearch International Ltd., Dallas, TX.*
> - *David Ford, President and Chief Executive Officer, Interguard Corp. of Guardian International, Auburn Hills, MI.*

They are all dead. And they all died in the same place at the same time: an April 1996 plane crash in Croatia on an official trade mission led by Ron Brown, United States Secretary of Commerce.[i]

Were these organizations ready for the sudden loss of their chief executives?

Succession Planning is a key aspect of Business Continuity Planning (BCP). BCP "identifies [an] organization's exposure to internal and external threats and synthesizes hard and soft assets to provide effective prevention and recovery for the organization, whilst maintaining competitive advantage and value system integrity".[ii] It is also called *business continuity and resiliency planning* (BCRP). This allows:

- The organization to be prepared to deal with sudden losses of key people.
- A continuing supply of qualified, motivated people to fill key positions.
- Reduced time and expense filling vacancies because the talent has already been identified and prepared.

"Grooming your replacement" is no longer an adequate solution to a succession policy. The challenge is not to merely replace managers and directors as they leave the organization, but to develop the best possible managers to meet the changing requirements of your organizational strategy.

Many NPOs claim they do Succession Planning; the reality is that most do not.

A primary challenge for organizations and businesses is to continue developing broadly experienced and seasoned managers in a way that is simple, practical, meaningful and fair. Meeting this challenge shifts focus to a talent pool, rather than to individual backups for key positions. It also allows for greater flexibility in preparing succession plans across departmental/functional lines.

Ideally, criteria for assessing managerial candidates and for guiding succession and development planning should be based on an analysis of supply (existing employees, key staff skills, and candidates) and demand (the NPO's requirements for staff). This analysis is outlined in the following chart.[iii]

Succession Planning Process

Inputs: Supply and Demand Information   **Outputs**: Plans to Meet Requirements

People

Candidate Data (Supply)
- Biographical data
- Skills and competencies
- Performance data
- Career Interests
- Planned retirement

Individual Development Plans
- Training and development
- Broadening and testing experiences

Position

Succession Requirements (Demand)
- Projected organizational and staffing needs
- Skills and competencies
- Job descriptions

Succession Plans
- Summaries of candidate availability and readiness
- Plans for meeting shortages (recruitment plans, accelerated development)

Management Review and Discussion

Replacement Planning versus Succession Planning

There is a difference between individual replacement planning and broader succession planning. Replacement planning concentrates on immediate needs and a snapshot assessment of the availability of qualified candidates for key management vacancies.

In contrast, succession planning is more concerned with longer term needs and the cultivation of a supply of qualified talent to meet those needs.

Succession planning involves a more intensive management review of job requirements, changing organizational needs, candidate information, appraisal information, and the specific developmental interests and choices of the candidates. It also calls for more systematic planning for the broadening of individual career potential.[iv]

Variable	Replacement Planning	Succession Planning
Time Frame	0 – 6 months	6 – 36 months
Resources	Best candidate available at the time	Candidates with best development potential
Level of Planning	Selection and placement of the preferred available candidate	Identification of high potential candidates well in advance
Selection Focus	Vertical line of succession within department, or external search	Development of a general talent pool
Development Plans	Immediate on-the-job training for new replacement	Extensive development planning with specific plans and goals set for each person in advance
Decision-Making	By Executive Director and a small interview panel	Development plans are the result of input and discussion from multiple managers
Candidate Evaluation	Past performance on job Demonstrated competence Career progress to date Interview panel	Multiple evaluations over time by different managers on varied job assignments

Key Positions

Succession Planning applies not just to executives and senior management positions, but to all key positions. Key positions are not always obvious. They are positions that have significant importance in the strategic and operational decisions that affect organizational success.

They are usually the top positions, but not always. They can be found in every department; for example, in production, distribution, systems, purchasing, programs, service, membership, and client liaison. A key position meets the following criteria:

- It performs critical tasks / actions.
- The organization would suffer if the function did not happen.
- It requires a vital specialty or expertise.
- It is involved in core business processes and/or mission-critical projects.
- It has geographical uniqueness.

Ask the following questions in order to assess and identify key positions in your NPO:

Criteria	Considerations
Mission	Is the position a key contributor to the organizational mission?
Leadership	Is this a leadership position?
Critical Function	Does the position perform tasks critical to vital functions? Does the position solely hold important corporate knowledge?

Criteria	Considerations
Essential Position	Would the organization suffer if this position was not filled? Would the sudden absence of an incumbent create a rapid breakdown in operations?
Specialization	Does the position involve a vital specialty or expertise?
Staffing / Turnover	Is the position vulnerable to high turnover due to high demand in the market? Would the position be difficult to fill (in time, effort and cost)? Would a long orientation / training period be required?

What are the truly key positions in your NPO? They are the ones you absolutely, positively can't live without.

Critical Success Factors

Successful succession plans and approaches incorporate the following factors:[v]

- Senior executives communicate the importance of succession planning as an organizational priority and are actively involved.
- Succession planning is aligned with business plans and to the broader HR planning process, including performance, development, learning, and recruitment.
- A fair, accessible, and transparent process is used.
- Planning extends to all levels of the organization rather than just to senior executive positions.
- Employees are assessed through multiple sources of data.

- Experiential learning is encouraged and is supported by coaching and evaluation of progress.
- A range of developmental activities is employed, individually tailored to address gaps in skills and competencies.
- Competencies and skills for key positions are reinforced in HR systems such as recruitment, learning, development, and performance management.
- The realization of employment equity and diversity goals is ensured.
- A good communications plan is in place.
- Managers and employees participate in workshops and information sessions to learn about the succession planning process.
- Tools that support the succession planning process are easy to use and accessible.
- The planning process is ongoing, monitored, evaluated, and refined.

Action Plans

NPOs need to consider their succession planning needs, create an awareness of them as a priority among directors and managers, and introduce new ways of thinking on this subject. Specifically:

- Adopt a corporate philosophy of management development.
- Identify a director-level corporate champion for Succession Planning (not the Director of HR).
- Develop a Succession Planning strategy statement.
- Incorporate management development into the broader training/learning program regime.
- Systematically identify a series/program of developmental assignments and incorporate this pro-

gram into business and workforce planning.

- Establish an annual management succession planning and review process (conduct management depth reviews) in which directors:
  - Individually present an analysis of their management talent supply and planned development activities.
  - Collectively identify high potential succession candidates.
  - Examine short-term replacement availability for key positions.
  - Prepare long-term development plans for succession candidates.
- Develop guidelines for a uniform approach to performance appraisals and the assessment of career development needs.
- Implement the required training and development programs.
- Review the process every year.

Notes

i William J. Rothwell, *Effective Success Planning: Ensuring Leadership Continuity and Building Talent From Within* (New York: AMACOM, 2001).
ii D. Elliot, E. Swartz and B. Herbane, "Just Waiting for the Next Big Bang: Business Continuity Planning in the UK Finance Sector," *Journal of Applied Management Studies* Vol. 8 (1999).
iii James W. Walker, *Human Resource Planning* (New York: McGraw-Hill, 1980).
iv Ibid.
v Treasury Board of Canada Secretariat (Ottawa, 2010).

8

Human Resources Outsourcing

Buy or Rent?

Effective management of the Human Resources function is critically important to the health of every non-profit organization. Executive Directors often complain that people issues are their number one priority. Unfortunately, due to competing demands and staff shortages, HR is often ignored or under-resourced.

Human Resources Outsourcing (HRO) is a tool used to manage small organizations. Instead of having internal staff perform HR activities and functions, HRO delegates HR to an outside service provider. The HR tasks are performed by a professional service provider on a part-time (for example, 1 to 2 days a week) contract basis, while the non-profit organization retains authority over these tasks.

When Should HRO Be Used?

HRO should be used when:

- High quality HR services are required for properly managing internal human capital but are not internally available.
- Senior management finds that they have neither the time, expertise or resources to deal with HR activities such as recruiting, staffing, compensation, training and development, retention, and employee relations.

Why Should NPOs Outsource HR?

Outsourced HR can be more efficient, effective, and cost reducing!

HRO allows internal staff to spend more time and energy on tasks that utilize their primary competencies in order to better manage the organization. The organization can benefit from cost savings as a result of the outsourced HR functions, which are of higher quality and timelier than if completed internally by reluctant senior managers.

An external service provider complements/strengthens/supports the senior management team by providing previously lacking or weak HR competencies which often include superior knowledge, innovation, an outside viewpoint, and legal compliance.

The Doctor is In

The part-time HR service provider is like Lucy in the Peanuts comic strip. She arrives on site, hangs out the IN sign, and waits for the customers to arrive.

This doesn't always happen. The customers don't always arrive. On our first HRO project the staff stayed away. The organization was an NPO that never had an HR function. After a few days, one of the employees timidly approached our consultant and asked, "What exactly is it that you do?" We had naively assumed that everyone knew what an HR manager does.

In subsequent HRO assignments, we sent out a staff communiqué outlining the full range of HR services (see Chapter 2 – HR Strategy). It still takes several weeks for management and staff to warm up to the idea. Once that happens, Lucy's schedule is always full.

What is the HRO Process?

The HRO process includes, but is not limited to, the following steps:

1. Assign a lead who will be responsible for managing the human capital of your organization. This

person is often the Executive Director or Director of Finance and Administration.

2. Compare current in-house processes and costs against the processes and costs of outsourcing.

3. Determine your expectations for outsourcing in order to achieve goals and objectives.

4. Identify HR activities or functions that can and should be outsourced.

5. Prepare a Request for Proposal (RFP) to help qualify service providers.

6. Review the responses to your RFP and research / reference check potential vendors.

7. Select a vendor that is the best fit with your organization and your needs.

8. Negotiate the contract terms with the chosen vendor, including timeframe of contract.

9. Develop a transition plan that considers the impact on current staff and operations.

10. Monitor, manage, and evaluate the performance of the service provider while ensuring compliance with contract terms.

What Are the Concerns With HRO?

A common concern with outsourcing is the challenge of implementing the transition to an external service provider as well as maintaining proper relations with them. Organizations may fear the service provider lacks confidentiality or knowledge regarding your sector.

A common fear among organizations that are new to outsourcing is the loss of internal knowledge and capability to perform the HR activities or functions after the outsourcing contract has expired. A final common concern is that the cost savings will not occur as expected.

How to Overcome HRO Concerns

- Talk to other NPOs that are currently using HRO about their successes and issues (if any).
- Carefully check the references of your service provider and the assigned resource.
- Ensure that contract terms and conditions are clearly spelled out.
- Give yourself an out – include a clause for immediate termination of the contract on your part for any reason without cancellation penalties.
- Provide early and effective communication to all employees and stakeholders in order to discuss the reasons for the change and the importance of cooperation.
- Carefully introduce the HRO service provider to employees and explain its role.
- Have the service provider conduct an initial HR Diagnostic study and prepare a report on the state of HR programs within your organization. This report will help the provider focus on immediate priorities, manage expectations, address areas of greatest need, and foster a common understanding regarding priorities.

Conclusion

HRO is simple, accessible and affordable. It can be a beneficial tool for any organization as long as it is a good fit, and planned for and implemented properly.

Appendix I

How to Speak HR

An NPO Reader's Guide to the Mystical World of HR Speak

What Real People Say	What HR People Say
Going to school	Enhancing Human Capital
Resume	Curriculum vitae (CV), Skills Inventory
Getting a Job	Staffing: Recruitment, Selection, Placement, TOS (Taken on Strength)
Getting a job because of my race, color, or gender	Affirmative Action, EEO (Equal Employment Opportunity), Employment Equity
Not getting a job because of my race, color, or gender	Discrimination
Not hiring men to work in the women's locker room	Bona Fide Occupational Qualification (BFOQ)
Having a job	FTE (Full Time Equivalent)
First day at new job	Orientation, Onboarding

The NPO Dilemma: HR and Organizational Challenges in Non-Profit Organizations

What Real People Say	What HR People Say
Knowing how to do my job	Competencies
Getting stuck with more work	Job Enrichment
Getting told what to do	Management by Objectives
"Good job, Tim"	Performance Management
"Good job, Boss"	360 Degree Feedback
Getting in trouble for coming in late	Progressive Discipline
Working a second job at night	Moonlighting
Being happy at work	Employee Engagement
Skipping a day's work	Absenteeism
Getting paid	Compensation
Big pay for the boss	Executive Compensation
Getting paid fairly	Internal Equity, External Equity, Employee Equity
Getting a raise	COLA (Cost of Living Adjustment), Merit Pay, Lift (British term)
Paying women the same as men	Pay Equity
Being at the top of my salary range	Red Circled
Having a few perks	Total Rewards Strategy
Flirting with Susan (or George)	Sexual Harassment, Personal Harassment
Having a wheelchair ramp on the sidewalk	Reasonable Accommodation
Nerds in the office	Knowledge Workers
Big pay for nerds in the office	Hot Skills Bonus
Working from home	Telecommuting
Wearing jeans on Friday	Business Casual Dress Code
Getting sent to another country	Expatriate

What Real People Say	What HR People Say
Bringing my wife / husband with me	Trailing Spouse
Having my job sent to another country	Offshoring
Having my job sent to another company	Outsourcing
Taking a training course	Continuous Learning
Taking several training courses	Talent Management
Getting the boss's job	Succession Planning
Getting laid off	Job Displacement, RIF (Reduction in Force), Pink Slip, Right Sized
Having my job grade, title, duties or status reduced	Demotion
Quitting my job	Voluntary Termination
Quitting becaused I was demoted	Constructive Dismissal
Walking away and never coming back	Job Abandonment
A bunch of people quitting, getting fired or retiring	Attrition, Turnover
Getting fired	Involuntary Termination, SOS (Struck Off Strength)
Getting fired for stealing, or punching the boss	Just Cause
No sex	Gender Neutral

Appendix II

The Top Ten Mistakes in HR Management

Tales from the Front Lines of HR Consulting

As Human Resources consultants, we work on the front lines of HR management. We are engaged on a regular basis with a variety of organizations: large and small, and from every sector. We have had the privilege of observing (and learning from) the very best HR practices and their successful outcomes. At the other end of the spectrum, we have been exposed to situations where we shake our heads in disbelief.

As a result, we have learned a lot. In this appendix we share with you a summary of our observations and findings over the years, and provide a checklist of the major pitfalls to avoid in your organization. No names are included, to protect the innocent, and the guilty.

1. Not Having a Plan

If we asked the first five employees who walk by your office door to tell us "What business are you in?" would they all give us the same answer? If your business were a Roman oar-driven galley, would all the rowers be rowing in the same direction? Or, would your ship be going around in circles?

We have seen organizations where employees do not know the core corporate objectives because management never told them. We have seen places where the organization charts are confidential and not shared with staff.

Our advice: you need a business plan (as any banker will tell you). You need a corporate strategy. You need an organizational model that depicts your work structure and is aligned to your business plan. All of these items need to be regularly updated and communicated to all levels of staff.

2. No Job Descriptions

We once heard a company CEO, in a business where there were no job descriptions, glibly state that "If my staff don't know what their job is, they have a problem." Our (tactfully unstated) response was "No, if your employees don't know what they are supposed to be doing, YOU have a problem." This approach is not bureaucratic; it is good business.

Job descriptions are the bedrock of any HR program. They spell out how the business and programs of the organization will be accomplished. They are invaluable tools in recruiting (job ads), new employee orientation, training, compensation and performance management.

Our advice: write them. They don't have to be long. Spell out the job title, reporting relationship, summary (or overview) of the role, a list of tasks and responsibilities, and the required skills and qualifications.

3. Hiring the Wrong People

An old adage has it that managers make up their mind about a candidate within the first 30 seconds of the interview. This may have some truth to it, but hiring by feel is plain wrong. Subjective impressions do not work. Many managers wing it, without a plan or any training. The majority of hiring managers we talk to in well known organizations (with HR departments) have never had a briefing on Human Rights and Interviewing.

Our advice: know the job you are hiring for. Know the organization's requirements. Create an Employee Referral Program. Hire for attitude, not just aptitude. Learn behavioral interviewing techniques. Know your human rights obligations. Use semi-structured interviewing guides. Be honest about the work environment and expectations. Involve others in the process. Conduct effective reference checks. Watch out for infatuation. Don't hire out of laziness or desperation.

4.　Not Getting Rid of the Wrong People

Managers hate to fire people. They debate, ponder, worry, procrastinate and agonize over it. Their angst is palpable. They hire consultants to tell them what to do – and then ignore the obvious advice. They put up with extraordinarily poor performance because (as I was once told) they don't have the chutzpah to make the required decision.

The rest of the organization watches in bewilderment as the poor performer drags everyone else down waiting for management to do something. The most relieved person in the world is a manager the day after they've fired someone. The weight is off their shoulders.

Our advice: flag poor performance early on. Advise the employee what they are doing wrong and how to correct it. Provide support and training. Follow up. Document it. Advise the employee of the consequences if the behavior continues. Introduce progressive discipline. Get some advice. Obtain input and guidance from others. If the problem persists, make a decision. Design an appropriate termination package and exit the employee.

5.　Failing to Engage

Does your work environment enable a sufficient and sustainable workforce in support of corporate objectives? To put that in plain English – are your staff happy campers? If morale is low, productivity suffers. If your organization is not productive, then your clients and stakeholders (in turn) will also not be happy campers.

Similar to real estate, where location reigns, the three most important words in employee relations are: "Communicate, communicate and communicate." "I don't know what's going on around here" is a major employee concern. Yet, "I don't have time" is the number one refrain we hear from managers about why they don't engage their staff.

Our advice: treat your staff as you would like to be treated. Tell them what is going on (and not going on) regularly. Ask for their input. Conduct Employee Satisfaction surveys. Carefully measure your retention and turnover rates. Conduct exit interviews; when staff leave you should know why.

6.   Paying Too Much or Too Little

Paying your employees too much is a waste of money. Paying them too little is also a waste of money since it can lead to turnover and increased recruiting, hiring and training costs. Paying new employees whatever they ask for – which we occasionally see – has been called Wild West management, with a similar body count.

How do you know what the going rate is for every position in your organization? How can you ensure fairness among employees, between different job levels, and with the external labor market? If you fail to do any of these – it will cost you money.

Our advice: write job descriptions. Use a job evaluation method to classify your jobs into levels or grades. Obtain wage and salary survey information (from the government, free web sites like Salary Wizard, or compensation survey firms). Determine where you wish to pay relative to the market averages. Establish pay bands (salary ranges). Pay your staff within the ranges. Communicate your Pay Policy.

7.   Failing to Recognize

In our arduous path through grade school, high school and university there is always one constant – feedback. We know how we are doing (even when we don't want to know). Everything we do is observed and graded. Then, we enter the workforce and (often) there is silence. The feedback ends.

People need to feel appreciated for their work. Neglecting to recognize and reward good performance can lead to morale issues and future attrition.

Our advice: pay attention. Tell your staff how they are doing. As Ken Blanchard said in *The One Minute Manager*, "catch your employees doing something right," and praise them. It can be as simple as saying thank you. Explore other reward and recognition options.

8.   Mismanaging Performance Appraisals

The annual performance appraisal is an event dreaded by most managers. In many organizations appraisals are a bureaucratic exercise in advanced "form filling-outing." HR is the police department driving this phe-nomenon, only satiated once all the papers are complet-ed and appropriately filed away. This may sound like "old HR," but we still see it regularly. In an effort to minimize workload and avoid conflict, managers often inflate the ratings of average or poor workers, or simply check the middle box in every scale.

Faced with this situation, a new Director of HR in one large public institution blew up the process. He de-clared a moratorium and cancelled all appraisals for two years. He used this interregnum to rebuild the concept from the ground up. While this approach may have been overkill, the key point is that performance appraisal is not about the form. It is about the employ-ee and their supervisor having a conversation on how the employee is performing relative to expectations.

Our advice: conduct the appraisals regularly. Keep them simple. Never forget that the primary goal is to pro-vide feedback. Educate your managers on this process.

9.   Not Having Rules of Engagement

The inconsistent application of policies drives employees crazy.

You're a busy and harried manager. Susan asks you if she can have next Friday off to help a friend prepare for a wedding. She will make up the time. You say okay. You then immediately forget about that decision. Your staff, however, do not. Three weeks later, Jane asks you the same question. You say no: "Sorry, we're too busy." The end result is predictable.

Our advice: create an Employee Handbook (if you don't have one already). Write down all of your HR policies, practices and rules in a straightforward reader-friendly manner. Introduce the handbook to all employees. Provide a copy to all new employees, and guide them through it. The consistent answer to Susan's and Jane's question is on page 17 under Leave Policies.

10.   Ignoring the Importance of Training

We regularly come across three common training issues:

i)   Employees are too busy to take training (or so their managers say). Staff are too invaluable in their roles and can't take "down time" for training. There is no one available to backfill employees.

ii)   Lack of a training strategy or plan. Identification of training needs is informal. Training is provided on an ad hoc basis.

iii) When times are tough and programs are being cut, the training budget is (still) the first casualty. It's an easy target with lots of funding sitting there and no immediate impact.

Your business is not static and neither are your staff. Your employees' skills need to be continually updated and refreshed in order to remain effective.

Our advice: learning, training and development systems and practices should be in place and aligned with your strategic goals and objectives. Establish a training budget that is within your means. Identify training needs – for both groups and individuals. Create Employee Learning Plans. Link them to Career Maps. Deliver training and track learning in a methodological manner.

About DataMotion Publishing

We Turn Experts into Authors

DataMotion Publishing was originally established to provide books, training materials and other published periodicals to Employment Practices Advisors, Inc., a human resources consulting firm.

Now a full service publishing business, DataMotion provides publishing and related support services to subject matter experts ranging from how-to guides, training materials and practitioners resources focusing on the human resources, legal and general business areas.

Services include:
* Manuscript Services
* Interior Book Design Services
* Cover Design
* Marketing and Promotion Services
* Book Website Development and SEO
* Registration Services

Our team of experts includes not only publishing and related professionals but also experienced writers and experts in the human resources, legal and business arenas.

www.datamotionpublishing.com
info@datamotionpublishing.com

www.ingramcontent.com/pod-product-compliance
Lightning Source LLC
Chambersburg PA
CBHW021559210326
41599CB00010B/521